12 Ways to get the most from Service That *Sells!*

1. Assign *Service That Sells!* to all of your managers to read in the next two weeks.

2. Ask them to write down the **fifteen best ideas** they see in the book as they read through it. At your next manager meeting, have each manager read his or her list.

3. Have your managers agree on the most significant ideas they got from reading the book and list them on a flip chart or piece of paper.

4. Have your managers prioritize the ideas at the meeting and then set a **specific timetable for implementation.**

5. Read pages 43 and 44 closely. Which of these eight steps are you **not** doing that you should be doing?

6. Assign pages 10-95 and pages 124-139 for every server and bartender to read. Ask them to write down the **ten best ideas they got from those sections. Assign a deadline for this "book report." Review the book reports at a server meeting and agree on an action plan for implementing the ideas.**

7. Make *Service that Sells!* required reading for every new manager, server, bartender or hostess in addition to your in-house training material. Design a twenty-question quiz that tests the basic material.

8. Use the role-playing exercise on page 52 to help your staff better learn your food and beverage items.

9. Design and post a chart, similar to the one on page 42 (using your menu items) to help transform your order-takers into salespeople.

10. **Assign the chapter on "Waste Watching" (pp 83-95) to your servers and kitchen crew.** Ask them to write down three ideas *they* have to control costs in your operation.

11. Assign each department (managers, servers, kitchen staff, bus staff, host staff, bartenders) to compile their own "Cycle of Service" based on the moments-of-truth unique to their jobs. Use page 124 as a model.

12. Use the 101 ways to sell more food and beverages (listed in the Appendix) as lesson plans for your next server training sessions.

First printing, January 1991.
10 9 8 7 6 5 4 3 2 1

ISBN 1-879239-00-0
PUB-513
Design & Graphics: Jennifer Gaul, Brian Rehder
Cover by Robert Bucciarelli Design, San Diego, CA
Printed in the United States of America

Service That *Sells!*

The Art of Profitable Hospitality

"You can have the best product in the world, but if you can't sell it, you've still got it."
— *Diamond Jim Brady, 1901*

Jim Sullivan & Phil Roberts

Pencom Press
Denver, Colorado

IYAD
WYAD,
YAG
WYAG!

(see page 151)

Acknowledgments

Our sincere thanks to:

Joe Armington
Jim Arnett
Michael Bartlett
Bob Basham
George Biel
Ken Blanchard
Norman Brinker
Doug Brooks
Micheal Charlton
John Cleese
Ken Cole
Buster Corley
Stephen Covey
Mark Danner
Jim Doherty
Robert E. Farrell
Larry Fineberg
Bob Fletcher
Jim Frye
Nick Galanos
John "Doc" Gardner
Rob Gillette
Marc Gordon
Charlie Greener
Frank Guidara
Hap Herndon
Ken Hill
Joe Hoff

Jerome Howard
Moses Howard
Smokey Hughes
Fred Hull
Greg Ibsen
Matt Jones
Pano Karatassos
Doug Lanham

Larry Levy
Mark Levy
Bruce MacDiarmid
Ron Magruder
Dick Marriott

John Martin
Tom Masi
Bill McLaughlin
Patsy Mellott
Joe Micatrotto
David Milligan
Bob Mock
Jim Moffa
Bob Morris
Peter Morton
Stan Novado
Hugh O'Neill
Bob Perkins
Tom Peters
Wolfgang Puck
Ed Rensi
Dick Rivera
Rob Robins
Darrel Rolph
Doug Roth
Jimmy Schmidt
Jon Sleik
Frank Steed
Alan Stillman
Chris Sullivan
Rick Van Warner
Teri Wheatley
Paul White

You've collectively inspired our point of view. Thank you for setting standards of excellence for our industry.

Thank you.

Table of Contents
A seven course meal of knowledge

Service That Sells!

❖   What it is, who we are and what's in it for you

The Seven Courses of Hospitality

● ●
▼

▼ ▼ ▼ ▼

HOW TO FIND THE
HIDDEN TREASURE OF
LOST SALES

❖ The two great myths of foodservice today

❖ Eight good reasons why your servers should see themselves as salespeople

❖ How to double your tips, your sales and your service

❖ The art of "soft" selling

Step #2: Know your products

❖ Soup du what?

❖ What will it take for me to get you in this new car today?

❖ You gotta know it if you're gonna sell it

❖ When the guest drinks better, **you** drink better

❖ "I'm not a flesh eater!"

❖ Can you top this?

Step #3: "Guide" your customers

❖ Why you need to guide your guests

❖ What you can learn from Batman, Robin and Hamlet

❖ Understand that "six" sells!

❖ How to "read" a customer

❖ Selling out of sequence: Don't give up the ship

❖ Are you "in the weeds" again?

❖ Ready? Fire. Aim!

❖ Action plan for teaching your servers how to "guide" their guests

Step #4: Use the right words

❖ What are the right words?

❖ Swami Sullivan's guide to creating mental pictures

❖ People remember the first and last thing you say

❖ Things you must *never* say to your guests

▼ ▼ ▼ ▼

▼   ▼   ▼   ▼

❖ The two-bite checkback
❖ Action plan for defining the customer contact points in **your** restaurant

FOREWORD!

*There is no foreword.
Nobody reads forewords to
books anyway. Besides, you've
got a restaurant, bar or
hotel to run, and we've got
1,001 ways to make it more
profitable. So let's stop wasting
time and get on into it....*

— The Authors

Introduction

Why you should read this book

Understanding how to operate a successful restaurant or bar is a lot like having a hangover. You can talk about it or read about it, but until you experience it, you just don't know what it's like.

Until someone actually discovers the secret to "The Perfect Foodservice Operation," there will always be a restaurant consultant, ex-waiter, "one man institute," retired psychologist or professor who thinks he or she has a better way to run your operation.

• •

"Those who can, do. Those who can't, teach. And those who can't teach become gym instructors."
— *Groucho Marx*

• •

Maybe they *have*, and maybe they haven't. But one thing we know for sure: sooner or later, they'll write a book about it and ask us to buy it.

The foodservice business today is evolving quicker than a Cro-Magnon family in a Stanley Kubrick film. It changes *daily.* Customers have more choices, competition is heating up, the traffic patterns are shifting and what little money we *do* make, the government wants more of. We believe it's imperative that you be *in* this business if you're gonna be *on* top of it or tell us how to do it. In other words, well *done* is better than well said!

Here's our promise: Unlike most authors, we won't tell you that it's going to rain.

This book is about how to build the ark.

▼   ▼   ▼   ▼

Why we wrote this book

We wrote this book because we *had* to. We couldn't find a common sense book on hospitality management that discussed the realities of both service *and* sales management. So we wrote down what we knew, researched what we didn't, and put it all together here. It's a fact of life that the best restaurateurs are shameless thieves. So here's our guarantee: Not all the ideas in this book are original, but what we've borrowed is the best. After all, imitation is the sincerest form of foodservice!

Our collective restaurant experience has spanned nearly every position.

You'll find *this* book different and effective because what we have to say is based on daily application, not "theory." We own and operate five successful high volume independent theme restaurants in Denver, Colorado, doing business as Premier Ventures. We've been in business since 1974 and our annual gross sales exceed $16 million, with virtually no media advertising.

Our collective restaurant experience has spanned nearly every position: dishwasher, buser, cook, host, server, accountant, bartender, trainer, manager, marketing director, district manager, director of operations and owner. We've worked in nearly every kind of foodservice operation: institutional and contract feeding, fast food, full service, chains, independents, hotels, you name it: from Brew 'n Burger to Steak and Ale. From Dairy Queen to Burger King. From Holiday Inn to Village Inn. From Fairmont Hotels to Fenway Park. From sea to shining sea, if there's one thing we've learned it's this: *There are only two things to worry about in the hospitality business: one, that things will never get back to normal, and two, that things already have!*

Who we are

Publications such as *Time, Newsweek, Cosmopolitan, Playboy, Esquire, Glamour, The Wall Street Journal, Nation's Restaurant News, Top Shelf, Hotel/ Motel Management, Restaurant Business, Nightclub and Bar, Restaurant Hospitality, Forbes, Business Week,* and *Inc.* have all featured our restaurants or our training programs on their pages. *Restaurants & Institutions* magazine recently chose our operations as the best managed independent restaurant group in the country and as one of 1993's top 20 "Concept Creators." This constant media attention created a lot of interest in our management programs, policies and procedures behind the scenes. Many of our colleagues (and competitors) wanted to know our "secret," so in 1985 we started "packaging" and marketing our unique hospitality training seminars, manuals and custom made

• • • • • • • • • • • • • • • • • • • •
Restaurants & Institutions *magazine recently chose our operations as the best managed restaurant group in the U.S.*
• • • • • • • • • • • • • • • • • • • •

videos to other restaurants, bars and hotels nation-wide through a company we helped develop named Pencom, Inc., also located in Denver.

We're honored that great companies like *Visa, Chili's, Chi-Chi's, Pizza Hut, Applebee's, Bennigan's, Hard Rock Cafes, Burger King, Anheuser-Busch, Inc., Denny's, Houlihan's, Bacardi Imports, T.G.I. Friday's, Carrow's, Marriott, Olive Garden, Lettuce Entertain You Enterprises, Red Lobster, Hyatt-Regency, Perrier, Red Robin, Holiday Inns, Arby's, Miller Brewing Company, The National Restaurant Association, Sheraton, Dairy Queen, Sysco Foods, Four Seasons Hotels, Westin, ARA Services,* and over 5,000 independent restaurants, bars and hotels nationwide have all invested in our live training seminars, books, audiotapes, videotapes, or consulting services. Pencom now delivers over 170 live seminars every year in the service industry with over forty topics for both management and staff.

And while our live seminar presentations are al-ways updated with new information, we decided it was time to commit the "basics" to paper.

This book reflects many of the action plans, dis-cussions, exercises and skills that we present in our award-winning seminars. If you're interested in learning more about our live programs, there's more

• •

"The venture must follow the vision. It's not enough to stare up the steps, we must step up the stairs."

— *Albert Koons*

• •

information in the back of this book. But first, settle back, hunker down and buckle up. It's time for *Service That Sells!*

Read it and reap.

▼ ▼ ▼ ▼

Top Ten Customer Service Turnoffs

1. Auctioning food ("Okay, who gets the burger?").

2. Dirty plates in hand when greeting customers ("Hi, ready for dessert?").

3. Not knowing what they're drinking ("I think this is the Diet Coke....").

4. Messy back bar (sure sign of a messy bartender).

5. "Discussion groups" of three of four idle servers (if you have time to lean, you have time to clean).

6. Not acknowledging waiting guests ("It shouldn't be much longer").

7. Pouring coffee from a stained coffee pot ("No more for me, thanks").

8. Answering your phone with "Hold, please." (rude, rude, rude).

9. Greeting guests with a number ("Two?" Instead, smile and say "Hi! Two for lunch today?")

10. Seating guests at a table with a tip on it (makes them feel uncomfortable).

The Four Objectives of *"Service That Sells!"*
(for you type-A personalities)

1. To show you **do-able** (not theoretical) ways to **improve service** in your store, restaurant, bar or hotel.

2. To teach you (and your employees) how to **increase sales and tips** 5 percent to 25 percent in your operation **immediately.**

3. To give you dozens of ways to significantly **reduce wastes and control costs.**

4. To improve your training skills so that you can **effectively teach** your staff how to improve performance, productivity and profits in your operation.

OUR GUARANTEE

Whether you're running independent operations, franchises, bars, fast food locations, cafeterias, hotel restaurants, 600 casual theme units or department stores, this book will serve as an easy reference guide to a smoother operation, happier customers, better team building and higher profits.

COURSE 1: Appetizers
"To sell is to serve"

The *Forbes* magazine cover said it all: *"It's Supposed To Be a Service Economy ... So Where's the Service?"* It's no secret that there's a service crisis in our country today. Despite the plethora of books in the 1980s that pointed this out, very little was done — short of adopting the slogans — to actually improve service delivery. **Service today is worse than it's *ever* been.** Witness, if you will, our collective service nightmare....

• •

> *"See no evil, hear no evil, speak no evil, and you'll never work for the customer service department."*
> — *Bob Snyder*

• •

You're on a flight. This disembodied voice on the overhead speaker informs you that your meal selection includes a choice of tuna salad or lasagna. Since you're watching your weight, you decide you'll request the tuna salad. By the time the flight attendants reach your seat they inform you that the only meal choice left is lasagna. You politely decline the lasagna, understanding that the demand was greater than the supply. You can always grab a tuna salad later at the hotel. No problem.

Forty-five minutes later you stroll to the back of the plane to visit the bathroom. While waiting for an opening, you glance at the rear galley where three flight attendants are standing, busily eating their lunch. You do a double-take, not because of *how*

▼   ▼   ▼   ▼

they are eating, but because of *what* they are eating: tuna salad!! No ... your tuna salad! You start the "slow burn." Your mind testily poses some rhetorical questions: *"Who paid $512 for the round trip airfare and who didn't? You or the flight attendant? Who's eating your meal and who's going without food?"* Oh well. No sense getting all worked up about it, you tell yourself. They

● ● ● ● ● ● ● ● ● ● ● ● ● ● ● ● ●

You can tune a piano ...

● ● ● ● ● ● ● ● ● ● ● ● ● ● ● ● ●

probably had a good reason for serving themselves instead of you ... right? Next month's Sunday paper details the dismantling and sale of that airline to a smaller competitor. Somehow, you're not surprised.

Two days later you are spending a frustrating morning in Bureaucracy Hell — the Motor Vehicle Department — to register a new car you recently purchased. There's a sign in the waiting area that says, "We're Committed to Excellence!" accompanied by a big yellow smile face. Taped to *that* sign is another: "Please take a number." You smile at the irony.

You've allotted 90 minutes for this chore; it's now an hour later and your "Take-a-Check" number reads 172. The monotone intercom voice just called

● ● ● ● ● ● ● ● ● ● ● ● ● ● ● ● ●

... you can't tuna salad

● ● ● ● ● ● ● ● ● ● ● ● ● ● ● ● ●

number 118. You groan and hunker down to wait. And *wait*. After sixty more minutes of squirming in an orange plastic chair, your number's finally called and you shuffle up to the so-called "service" counter. You face an "Iron Curtain" of four indifferent, unsmiling, departmental employees. Their "conversation" is little more than verbal anesthesia. "Civil servants" they're called, and you soon come to the conclusion that they are rarely either. A quick look at their faces confirms that you've found the collective inspiration for the whiskey sour. After paying $193.82 for the "privilege" of license plates and this civil abuse the cashier yells "NEXT!" You can't resist the temptation. *"Don't I get a 'thank you'?"* you ask her in exasperation. *"It's on your receipt,"* she sniffs. *"Who's next here???"*

Civil servants from Hell

You're at a shopping mall food court, hoping to grab a quick lunch. You pause in the "undecided patron safety zone," 30 feet back from two different counters. You're trying to settle on a burger and fries or the slice of pizza. The employees at the counter of the burger stand look off in the distance and grunt "Kelp you?" in your general direction. You try to think quicker. The pizza vendor offers his wares: "Kelp you over *here?*" You settle on the burger, stride to the counter and say "Can I have the burger, fries and a medium soft drink combo, please?" The response? "$4.19. Your number is 64." They look over your shoulder. "Kelp *you*, sir?" You feel like a wallet with a person attached. Mmm, mmm, mmm, now *that's* service ... NOT!

A quick look at their faces confirms that you've found the collective inspiration for the whiskey sour.

Must be "secret" service. Only they know what they're doing!

Are the examples above more often than not the style of service you've grown accustomed to? Every day we sally forth into the "Consumer Arena of Service Heaven" or "Service Hell," braced for battle, brimming with expectations, hoping for service excellence, but, more often than not, we end up receiving something closer to *service abandonment* instead. Everybody's read the books on "excellence" and "service" but—short of adding the words "excellent" and "quality" and "customer-driven" to their train-

▼   ▼   ▼   ▼

ing manuals — hardly anybody's *doing* anything about actually meeting the customer's expectations.

What do you *do* about bad service? Surveys tell us that most customers "vote" on it with their feet. They patronize someone else and never let the offending business know why. Can you blame them? **We** can't. Plus, statistics show that they'll tell at least twelve other people about it. Those twelve tell six others. Those six others tell three more each! *That's 300 people who'll hear about that bad service experience from a friend.* Every company wants "word-of-mouth" advertising, right? Wrong. You want *positive* word-of-mouth advertising!

Service excellence or abandonment.

If you're **in** the service industry, how difficult is it to put the customers' interests before your own? American businesses were able to charge taxpayers $600 for a toilet seat and $700 for a wrench. It seems like we *should* be able to get a tuna salad for $512 or a "thank you" from the Motor Vehicle person for a $193.82 piece of paper marked "Title"!

To improve your performance, profits and productivity in the hospitality business, remember three things:

▼

- ◆ Bad service happens all by itself, good service has to be managed.

- ◆ Great marketing ("We're committed to excellence!") can kill a bad business! ("Sorry, not my section.")

- ◆ Listen to your customers and then *DO* what they tell you to do!

▼   ▼   ▼   ▼

When's the last time you had too much good service?

After shoddy treatment by his waiter at a well-known Westside L.A. restaurant, a friend of ours asked to see the manager. The manager arrived with the greeting, *"What's the problem here?"* "Indifferent, rude and surly service," our friend said. "Impossible," sniffed the manager, "service is our middle name, sir!"

"Oh yeah?" our friend replied, "then 'BAD' must be your *first* name."

There's no question that service generally stinks in this country. The question is what are we gonna do about it? This rising bad service **awareness** is slowly evolving into bad service **intolerance** among consumers nationwide. They're mad as hell, and they're not gonna take it any more. Do you blame them? We don't. Everybody's out searching so hard for "excellence" these days that maybe we're forgetting to *serve* the person we're trying to be so "excellent" *for:* our customers.

How good are we, in the hospitality industry, at delivering **service that *sells?*** We've all gone out and had to much to eat or drink, but when's the last time you had *too much good service???* When did you *ever* hear someone say, *"The food is okay, but the service is great. Don't go there!"?*

We know that this message about the "Service Void" isn't new. Hundreds of self-styled service "gurus" are popping up out there every day, pounding pulpits on the lecture circuit and writing books about "the service crisis." They preach that those of us in service industries are "bad," that our customers want better service and it's **our** job to deliver it. Pretty startling revelation, huh? That'll be $19.95 please ($49.95 for hardcover, $695 for the video!).

▼ ▼ ▼ ▼

Look, write all you want about service but stop telling us *what* **the problem is, and start telling us** *how* **to do something about it.** We think it's necessary to point this out to the New Age Service Shamans, not out of malice, but because these nouveau gurus all avoid defining a fundamental point about service delivery: SERVE ALL YOU WANT, BUT IF YOU CAN'T MAKE IT SELL, YOU'RE OUT OF BUSINESS.

In other words....

Service: Hit or myth?

Have you ever stopped to think about what "service" really means? What is it? Can it be defined? (Forget Webster; as far as we know, **he** never worked flipping burgers, mixing drinks, selling clothes, listing real estate, or checking in hotel guests.) We define service simply as *"the manner in which the customer is treated."* It's a thing more often *felt* than seen. It's a magic act, an illusion, a **perceived** value that accompanies an exchange of goods for money. It can be good, bad or indifferent. The customer's service expectations are based on the **type** of product we've chosen to offer, the **price** of the product, the **environment** in which the product is being offered, and (most importantly) the **manner** in which the product is delivered.

• • • • • • • • • • • • • • •
Service is an illusion.
• • • • • • • • • • • • • • •

So what? Any "consultant" book, or the plethora of Tom Peters-tag-alongs can tell you that. But let's dig a little deeper into the bag of Service Definition. (Stick with us here. We want to take you from the "hole" to the entire donut.)

Where does "service" come from? *What's the motivation for any employee to provide service to a cus-*

tomer? Forget honor, pride and warm fuzzy feelings for now — that stuff comes later. The answer is **because we want them to *buy* something!**

Think about it. Don't shy away from this significant fact of business life. **ADMIT IT!** Why would anyone want to help or "serve" you in, say, a shoe store? What's the employee's motivation to pay attention to you? Why would they want to help you put your musky, smelly, stinky feet into three or four different pairs of shoes?

They're hoping you'll buy those shoes! The store manager hires that person based on the agreement

that they will suggest (and hopefully sell) shoes, socks, belts, shoe polish, clothes or whatever items the store offers to any and all customers who walk in the store. *Making the sale* is the ultimate desired result; "serving" the customer is a *means* to the end, not the end itself.

> • • • • • • • • • • • • • •
>
> *"Volume times zero isn't very healthy."*
> — Lee Iacocca
>
> • • • • • • • • • • • • • •

Service is something you do that expedites, or results in, a purchase, a sale or a return visit. Without "service" you can still make a sale ("self-serve" gas stations, for example). **But without sales, service cannot exist.** Service is sweet, *but it's sales that feed the bulldog.*

HEY! Are you mad as hell about shoddy service?

Do you have a service-related anecdote that you'd like to see in print? Call us at 1-800-247-8514 and tell us about it. We'll send you a free "Day in the Life of a Restaurant Manager" poster and credit you in the next edition!

Service is the handle. Sales is the pump.

Why do restaurants, bars or hotels fail and close their doors? Despite the popular notion to the contrary, "bad food" or "poor service" never caused a restaurant or store to shutter its doors.

The bottom line is that businesses fail every day *not* because they couldn't "serve" their guests but because *they couldn't cover their costs.* "Service" may create word-of-mouth traffic in your restaurant or bar but it's **making sales** that keeps the restaurant or business *open* and the staff *employed.* "Service" alone won't sustain any company, even a "not-for-profit" one.

Service *and* sales (combined with effective cost control) *is* what makes and keeps a restaurant successful, your staff employed and your business in operation. Service is the handle. Sales is the pump. Remember us asking when the last time was that you received too much good service? Here's another good question for you: ***When's the last time you or your restaurant made too much money?***

Service is the most important thing you "sell."

If your answer is "the Twelfth of Never," read on. And hey, don't get us wrong; we're not suggesting that you ignore the importance of service in your operation. **Service is the most important thing you "sell."** *Service is your invisible product,* good service adds value to the purchase, and service is what ultimately brings your customers back. Nobody makes a "bad" *anything,* so service is the one thing you can always do better than your competitors, no matter how big their advertising budget is. But the premise of this book is simple: *selling is an integral part of the service process.* No business provides service without aiming for a pocketbook somewhere along the line.

Our friend John "Doc" Gardner has another way of putting it: ***"Business is what, if you don't have, you go out of!"***
Amen.

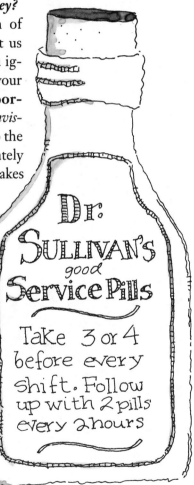

Dr. SULLIVAN'S good Service Pills

Take 3 or 4 before every shift. Follow up with 2 pills every 2 hours

▼   ▼   ▼   ▼

Nightmare on sales street

Why are so many people in the service industry in general or the restaurant, bar and hotel business in particular freaked out by the word "sell?" We wish we had a nickel for every server or bartender who said, *"No, no! Don't make me do it! Not the S-word! I'll serve all you want, but I don't want to sell! Aaaaugh!"* Thousands of waiters and waitresses — and managers — feel that

• • • • • • • • • • • • • • • • • • • •

How to save $45,000 a year.

• • • • • • • • • • • • • • • • • • • •

way. Why? They just don't get it. It's probably because the customer might decline their suggestion for a side of fries, an appetizer or dessert and they'll feel "rejected." Nobody likes that feeling. But our experience has shown that most servers shy away from selling because they don't know *how* to sell.

People are naturally skittish about anything they don't understand. And unfortunately, many restau-

rateurs spend little or no time on effective employee sales training along with their service training. Some people are afraid of the dark and some are afraid to leave it. (If "ignorance is bliss," we know a lot of extremely happy restaurateurs out there!) As a result, the server's ingrained stereotype about selling being "pushy" — fostered by the image of the used-car salesperson — is reinforced daily by restaurateurs or hoteliers who tolerate order-takers on their staff.

We say "serve" all you want, but if you're not **selling** anything, you're out of business! Serve on. Be friendly. Open the door for your guests. Pull out their chairs. Smile. Use their names. All of these things are extremely critical. *But if they don't buy anything, you're out of business!* To prove the importance of sales training, the story goes that Marshall Field once went an entire year without buying anything that wasn't sold to him. He claimed he saved $45,000!

One waiter came up to us after an employee meeting and said, "*I* know why you guys are pointing out that suggestive selling raises our tips; it's really so that the restaurant makes more money."

Yes! Exactly! He was absolutely right! When the company succeeds, the employees succeed. We admit it! The best way to get to know your guests and

• • • • • • • • • • • • •
How customers benefit from selling.
• • • • • • • • • • • • •

make them comfortable is to talk to them. The best thing to talk to them about is your food and beverage. After all, that's why they're here. And the best way to get your customers to buy what they came in for is to train your servers to sell it to them. Anyone can be an "order-taker." It requires *service to sell.*

▼   ▼   ▼   ▼

The art of the "soft" sell

Please understand that the kind of selling we're talking about here is suggestive selling, **soft selling,** not *"Used-Car-Salesman-Pushy-Loud-Pinkie-Ring-Checkered-Coat-Platform-Shoes-Buy-or-Die!"* selling.

Suggestive selling means helping guests make decisions that are good for them. It's recommending what's *good* on the menu, asking *questions* about what guests are in the mood for, and then *helping them choose* the food or beverage they'd like. Suggestive selling is nothing more than recommending (not "pushing") specific extras, appetizers, sides, desserts and beverages. Suggesting specific items shows guests they're worth your time; it's perceived as better service.

Bottom line: you and your servers have *everything* to gain from suggestive selling (higher sales, bigger tips, better service, more business) and *nothing* to lose (the guest says "no thanks!") That's what's in it for *you* to suggestively sell, but what's in it for your customers? Bring on...

The "garbage burger"

The more food and beverage you sell, **combined with controlling your overhead,** the more likely your restaurant is to be profitable. The more your waitstaff sells, the higher their check average and the better their tips or, if you're a fast food operation, the quicker the raise. Obviously, owners, managers and servers directly benefit from suggestive selling. But how does the most important person in your restaurant — your guest — benefit? Simple. The more the server suggests, the *less* the customers

• • • • • • • • • • • • • •
Seeing without seeing.
• • • • • • • • • • • • • •

have to ask for. And the less effort customer has to spend, the better they enjoy their overall experience and the more satisfied they are with the service they received at your restaurant. Here's a true story from Jim Sullivan's Real Life Casebook to better illustrate this point:

After an evening of post-softball-league celebrating with my teammates, I went to eat lunch at a full-service restaurant famous for its hamburgers and ribs. The smiling waitress looked me in the eye and said, "You look like you could use something to eat!"

"You're right," I said. "I want one of your steak burgers. Medium, please."

"You like Swiss cheese?" she asked with a nod. "Sure," I said. "And how 'bout bacon and mushrooms? We use fresh sliced mushrooms sautéed in burgundy wine."

"Yeah, that sounds good!" I liked her style.

"Okay ... a juicy steak burger ... medium ... and uh, whatta ya think ... we'll add the bacon, our burgundy mushrooms, cover it with Swiss and put it in the broiler until that cheese melts all over it. Lettuce, tomato and a slice of red onion on a grilled homemade sourdough roll. It's *the* best burger in town. Sound good?"

Good? I've gotta tell you I could *see* that hot, juicy bacon mushroom burger on the spatula going in the salamander with the Swiss melting all over it! Good? It sounded *great!* I closed my menu and told her that that's *exactly* what I wanted. But she had one more good idea.

"All right, now you've got to try a cup of our homemade chili on the side. You can dip your burger in it on every bite. We call it a

'garbage' burger. It sounds different, but it's really good. I'm having one later myself."

"Sounds messy," I said.

"I'll keep a fresh supply of napkins for you."

I smiled, "Sold!"

"Side of curly-cue fries to chase that burger down? They're a quarter more, but they're the best," she said, nodding her head. I agreed and asked for a glass of water.

"Perrier or 'House Water'?" I asked what the "house water" was.

How to make guests tip more.

"Tap," she said with a smile. I opted for the Perrier. She left smiling. I was too.

How word-of-mouth advertising spreads

Well, that burger was fantastic! It was juicy, gooey, delicious and fun to eat. It cost me $6.25 instead of $3.95, but it was worth *twice* that much in terms of the experience, the value and the Awe-of-Service-Well-Done feeling it created in me. (It was worth four times as much to her. I left a $3.00 tip. The plain $3.95 burger would have netted her about 75¢ at 15 percent!)

But wait. There's more.

When I went back to work I told two of my co-workers, Tito and George, about the great burger I had. I described it just like the waitress described it to me. They resolved to go there for lunch the next day to check it out. My waitress had used "service that sells" on me and created two new customers for that restaurant through my unsolicited advertising!

WORD of MOUTH
Guaranteed to Spread
at least 300x's!!!

▼   ▼   ▼   ▼

How word-of-mouth advertising fails

I saw my associates later in the week and asked how they enjoyed their burgers.

"Terrible," they said in unison. George looked as mad as a pig on ice with his tail froze in.

"What in the world did you see in *that* place?" said Tito. "What do you mean?" I said. "Didn't you have that 'garbage burger', with the swiss and bacon and mush---"

"No, it wasn't on the menu," George grunted.

"Yeah, I know," I said, "The waitress tells you about it."

• • • • • • • • • • • • • • • • • •

Walking vending machines.

• • • • • • • • • • • • • • • • • •

"Our waitress didn't. We ordered burgers and that's just what we got," Tito said. "She didn't suggest anything. I tried describing it to her. I said, 'It has bacon on it.' She says, 'that's extra!' I said, 'Alright, fine, and it also has mushrooms and Swiss.' 'Those are extra, too!' she says. So then I said, 'I guess you can get a cup of chili on the side...'

"'GROSS!' she interrupts, 'That burger's not on our menu, I don't think,' and she stares at us. Suddenly she says, 'I'll give you guys a few more minutes,' and takes off to the kitchen or bar or somewhere. We ended up ordering a plain cheeseburger and fries. She seemed to be able to handle that."

"By the way," George added, "what did you see in that place anyway?"

True story, and the moral is:

❖ Server-suggested food and beverage always taste better than an "order-taker's" does.

❖ Consistent suggestive selling creates positive word-of-mouth business for your present and future customers that advertising can't buy.

❖ Inconsistent waitstaff training can create *negative* word-of-mouth advertising.

❖ Training *half* your staff to be salespeople and allowing the other half to be merely "order-takers" will cost you at least half your business!

The dollar cost of losing one guest

Earlier we told you that if someone has a bad experience in your restaurant because of poor or indifferent service, statistics show they'll tell **ten to twelve** *other* people — who weren't there — about how bad it was. Those *twelve* people will tell *six* others, and those six will tell *three* more people each. Total it up and that's *300 people who hear about that bad service experience through negative word-of-mouth advertising.* You may have lost a potential **300 new customers per day** by making one customer angry enough not to come back and tell a dozen of his friends not to, either. What does that negative feedback cost you every year in lost gross sales?

Multiply 300 people per day times 365 days a year and that's 109,500 customers per year times the dollar amount of your average guest check. Let's assume it's $8 per person. Ready? Take a breath and keep on reading....

That's **$876,000** in lost potential gross sales each year because you made **one** guest unhappy enough to not want to return! YIKES!

What if training your employees significantly reduces or eliminates the chances of poor or indifferent service, and therefore reduces the odds of people complaining to their friends

• • • • • • • • • • • • • •

How to lose 300 new customers per day.

• • • • • • • • • • • • • •

about it? Is it a cost-effective investment to improve the service and sales skills of your waitstaff? In other words....

Is that $876,000 in potential gross sales per year *flying* out of your pocket? Are you *sure* your training program is all that it can be? What if you took *one percent* or even ten percent of that potential sales figure and invested it to show Debbie, Errol, Felipe and Christy how to improve service, reduce waste, and sell more appetizers, wine and desserts? Do you think *that* would create a bigger return on investment than a $30,000 facelift for the dining room? Train now, renovate later. The former pays for the latter.

COURSE 1:
Introduction and "Appetizers" summary

Service does not exist without sales.
To sell is to serve.

Our guests are here to buy, not browse.

You can have the best product in the world, but if you can't sell it you've still got it!

Don't build up the reputation of your food, drinks or atmosphere without simultaneously investing in service and sales training of your staff.

Don't throw away a potential $300,000 in lost gross sales each year by tolerating order-taking.

Train everyone on your staff to be service-oriented salespeople.

Suggestive selling benefits everyone; the restaurant, the server and, most importantly, the guest.

● ●

"Anyone who eats three meals a day should understand why cookbooks outsell sex books three to one."
— *L.M. Boyd*

● ●

Teach your waitstaff that service and sales are synonymous.

When training servers, stress that not only do they make better tips, but the guest gets better service (relate the "Garbage Burger" story).

As many as 300 people hear about one bad service experience in your restaurant. Train to beat or eliminate the odds of this happening.

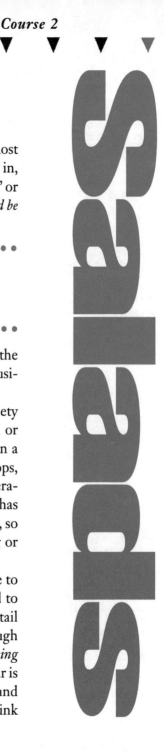

COURSE 2: Salads
"Lettuce sow, lettuce reap"

If we asked you to define what business most employees of the foodservice industry work in, you'd probably say the "restaurant" or "hotel" or "bar" business. And do you know what? *You'd be wrong!* That's not the business you're in.

• •

If you think you're in
the restaurant business
you're wrong.

• •

We're in the business of retail sales, not the "fast food," "restaurant," "bar," or "hotel" business.

Think about it. We "manufacture" a variety of products and merchandise in the kitchen or bar. Then we offer it for sale to customers in a "display and service" area known as countertops, tables or dining rooms. Unlike most retail operations, such as department stores, our product has a limited "shelf life" due to potential spoilage, so there's a greater sense of urgency for selling or "moving" our products.

A restaurant or bar is not merely "a place to eat or drink," but rather a building designed to accommodate, facilitate and promote the retail *sales* of food and beverage to customers through service. We provide service as a way of *making* sales to those customers. The restaurant or bar is a physical space. Our business is designing and using that space to make sales. Why do you think we call our restaurants "stores?"

▼   ▼   ▼   ▼

McDonald's versus Neiman-Marcus?
The difference between a restaurant and a department store

Once you begin to look at your restaurant or bar as a retail sales store you need to re-think the way you're managing it. Are you a floor manager or a sales manager? There are five distinct differences between selling in a restaurant or hotel and selling in a department store:

1. In a restaurant, or bar, we **both manufacture and sell** our product under the same roof.

TO SERVE IS TO SELL

You don't buy coal, you buy heat.
•
You don't buy circus tickets, you buy thrills.
•
You don't buy the paper, you buy the news.
•
You don't buy glasses, you buy vision.
•
You don't buy dinner, you buy sales and service.

2. **In a restaurant, or bar, we know that our customers are here to buy, not "browse."** Nobody comes in to "try on" a steak, a hamburger, a burrito or an omelette! Since your customers are here to buy, it makes sense to realize that **your staff is here to suggest and sell.**

3. In a restaurant or bar, our **customers may return as many as three times a day to spend money** (lunch, happy hour, dinner). This is not very likely in a department store unless you're a serious shop-a-holic! If a hamburger combo or a steak, a grilled chicken sandwich or pizza is suggested, prepared and served well, our guests *will* return for more — maybe as soon as tomorrow and the day after that. (Very few people will buy the same coat, shoes or hat four days in a row!)

> • • • • • • • • • • • •
> *"Every crowd has a silver lining."*
> — *P.T. Barnum*
> • • • • • • • • • • • •

4. Department stores provide service, but restaurants provide *hospitality:* a warm feeling resulting from feeding both the body and the soul.

5. More entertainers open restaurants and bars than department stores. Why? Cuz this is showbiz!

Marketing: It ain't how you get 'em, it's how you keep 'em!

Once the analogy between foodservice and retail sales is understood we can then differentiate between what we *do* and what we *should* be doing. First, we begin by making a distinction between our business's *function* and our *goal*. What is the **function** of the restaurant business? A trainer probably said it best in a video we saw:

- ❖ "Our **function** as a business is to **acquire** and **maintain** customers,"

- ❖ "Our **goal** is to be profitable."

••••••••••••
*What your staff
doesn't know.*
••••••••••••

We're willing to bet you the price of this book that if you asked your staff what the function of *your* restaurant or bar is, 99 percent of them (including managers) would confuse the function with the goal and reply *"To make money."* Most employees find it hard to believe that there are many months in a restaurant's year where the goal (to make money) is *never* achieved because the function (to find and keep customers) is never attained.

How do we *acquire* customers? By effective *external marketing* which can be defined as what we do to get people in our restaurants, like advertising, promotions and so on. How do we **maintain** or **retain** customers? Through effective *internal marketing* which is what we do to our guests once they're

••••••••••••••••••••••••
*"What if you train your servers to
be salespeople and they leave?
What if you don't and they* **stay?"**
— *Brad Huisken*
••••••••••••••••••••••••

in our establishments. It can be good, bad or indifferent. Obviously, we want to not only live up to our guest's expectations, but to consistently try to exceed them.

If you agree with this differentiation between a business's function and goal you must then ask yourself: "How do I successfully manage my business's *function* every day so that we will make money?" The answer is quite simply: **TRAINING**.

Why train?

❖ It's your crew members or staff — not the managers — who determine if you maintain your customers.

❖ Your staff will do as much or as little as you lead them to do.

Identify your unknown salespeople.

❖ The way you treat your employees determines how they'll treat your guests.

❖ The more you expect from a person the more you have to train them.

❖ **If the son swears ... strike the *father!***

A well-trained staff not only helps you acquire and maintain more customers, it helps you acquire and maintain better employees. And employees should be treated as our internal customers. Service is a level playing field. You may not be able to match your competition's advertising budget, but you sure as heck can train your staff as well or better than theirs. What do we train them to do? Read on.

Putting wind in your sales

Tell your staff about the "honor" of serving people all you want, but eventually the topic gets around to dollars and *sense*. They say money can't buy happiness ... but every hospitality employee *we* know says, *"Fork some over and watch me smile!"* The best way to justify raises is

for the employee to generate sales. The best way to earn bigger tips is to provide better service.

Seeing your restaurants or bars as retail sales operations means we need to see our *servers* as *commissioned salespeople* and manage *all* of our employees as *potential profit centers.* **Everyone who works for us is a salesperson** disguised as a server, bartender, host, hostess or cook.

Independent contractors....

As a matter of fact, everyone who works anywhere doing anything is a salesperson in one form or another! In a restaurant, we merely have different *departments* of salespeople, like counter help, waitstaff, bartenders, host staff, busers, managers and chefs. Let's focus now on the employees who deserve and require the most and best sales training: servers, bartenders, busers, host staff and managers.

Servers & bartenders

Servers and bartenders should be taught to see themselves as independent contractors. Your waitstaff's station, section or bar is their "territory." Guests "sign" their commission checks daily in the form of tips, repeat business and referred business. The restaurant takes all the risk and pays for all the upfront costs: table settings, utilities, insurance, flatware, napkins, food and beverage, etcetera. Your servers have nothing to lose and everything to gain.

The smart restaurateur realizes that servers aren't our only salespeople. Busers, host staff, foodrunners and expediters are all potential profit centers, too. Seeing all of your front-line employees as salespeople means you have a daily obligation to teach and train everyone to use service that sells.

> *"The four basic behaviors of service excellence: Look at me. Smile at me. Talk to me. Thank me."*
> — *Douglas Edwards*

The little buser that could....

It probably makes sense to you to think of your servers as salespeople. But how does training your bus staff or host staff have an impact on better service or higher sales? Good question! Consider this scenario: We were having dinner in a well-known Chicago restaurant. I flagged down a passing buser and asked him to please get our waitress.

What do you need, sir?" asked the buser, who looked all of 17 years old.

"Just another drink, please," I said. He asked what I was having. I told him a "vodka tonic."

"Did you want to try Absolut in that?" asked the buser.

"Sure..." I said, slightly stunned, *"Absolut would be great."* The buser told my waitress, and she brought the drink.

I was served quicker (and therefore better) and our waitress saved a step and made a better tip (and I assume the buser did also), all because someone took the time to invest some product knowledge training in their bus staff. As our friend Christopher O'Donnell says, *"The restaurant business is a series of opportunities and you either hit 'em or miss 'em!"*

▼ ▼ ▼ ▼

Selling from the front door

Don't forget to also invest training time and money in the *first* salesperson your guests meet ... your host or hostess.

For example, a hostess seats two of your guests and instead of just saying "Enjoy your dinner!" she says, *"We've got a great selection of wines by the glass listed here, and an incredible Mud Pie for dessert. Enjoy your dinner!"*

Hear the difference? By briefly pointing out specific beverages and food (wine and Mud Pie) this hostess has opened the "Window of Opportunity" for the server to follow up with another wine or dessert suggestion and most likely make the sale and higher tip! (Note: see Course 6 for a detailed list of the specific service behavior a good host or maitre'd provides.)

... it's the 10 percent we do differently that means success.

Could *your* buser, host or hostess perform his or her job in the same manner as the one in the above scenario? Do you think that the buser, host or hostess was *born* with that ability or were they *taught* that skill? Training all of your "frontliners" to know the menu and the right words results in better service, higher sales, and perhaps most importantly, sets your restaurant and bar apart from your competitors who don't. **Remember: 90 percent of all restaurants and bars do 90 percent of the same things the same way. It's the 10 percent we do differently that means success.**

▼ ▼ ▼ ▼

COURSE 2: Salads!
Lettuce sow, lettuce reap
summary

- The *function* of a restaurant is to attain and retain customers.

- The *goal* of a restaurant is to make money.

- Operating your restaurant like a retail sales store is the key to higher sales, lower turn-over (employees who make more money tend to stay around longer), better service and positive word-of-mouth advertising.

- Seeing, and managing, all of your employees as potential profit centers and salespeople reinforces their perception of your restaurant as a retail sales and service store.

- The more you expect from a person, the more you have to train them.

- Start coaching, teaching and training everyone on your staff as salespeople *today* and watch the results tomorrow.

"Welcome. Will that be 2 for dinner tonight?"

• •

"Remember the 10-10-10 rule. It costs a business **ten years** *and* **ten** *thousand dollars to acquire one customer that an untrained server can lose for you in* **ten** *minutes through rude or indifferent service."*
— *Greg Prokopchak*

• •

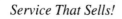

▼ ▼ ▼ ▼

COURSE 3: Entrees
"The meat of the matter"

How do you raise your guest checks one dollar (or more) per person?

Tuning into WII-FM or where's the hidden treasure in your restaurant? WII-FM is the number one *most* popular radio station in the world. Why? Because it means:

• •

What's In It For Me?

• •

Adult learners are more likely to listen, and hopefully learn new skills only after the teacher or trainer shows them what they stand to gain by listening or learning. How will they benefit? What will they get?

Let's start with restaurant or bar owners, operators and managers. We'd like to illustrate through a simple math exercise (don't worry, no quadratic equations or logarithmic tables are required!) what's in it for *you* to begin investing more time and money in training your waitstaff and bartenders to start seeing themselves as salespeople, not order-takers.

"What's In It" for owners, operators and managers to invest in sales training?

1. Write down your approximate daily customer count:

_____

2. Now, write down the number of days you're open:

_____

3. Multiply number two times number one:

_____

4. Add a dollar sign to the left of the answer from #3 above.

Look at that last figure long and hard. How'd you like to see that number added to your gross sales this year and *every* year without raising prices or doing any advertising? That's the Hidden Treasure of Lost Sales in your restaurant: the result of adding only *one dollar* to your per person check average! You don't have to be Indiana Jones to find it, it's hiding in your staff's ability (or inability) to merchandise your menu!

• • • • • • • • • • • • • • • • • • •

"No brain, no **headache.***"*
— *Duncan Bright*

• • • • • • • • • • • • • • • • • • •

What's a buck???

- a pitcher of Budweiser shared between *five* people,
- a *slice* of cheese or side of fries with a burger,
- *one* cup of coffee,
- *one* soft drink,
- a *glass* of juice,
- upgrading a vodka and tonic to *Absolut*, or a gin and tonic to *Bombay*,
- *four* guests sharing one $3.95 appetizer,
- a *cup* of soup,
- *one* $1.95 dessert split by *two* guests,
- *one* extra topping on a pizza,
- *one* $16 bottle of wine shared by four customers at every fourth table!

That doesn't sound too difficult, does it? It isn't. So now that we know what we stand to gain, let's look at how we have to train.

In this next section we're going to show you **how to teach** your servers, bartenders and host staff to smile, sell, serve and *get* those check averages up a dollar per person or more.

Remember, it may say "Joe's Restaurant" on the sign outside, but it's *Doug* and *Mary* and *Fred* and *Kathy* and *Sam* who are controlling the amplitude of the cash flow between the guest and Joe, the owner! The more you teach them, the more they learn. The more they learn, the better they earn.

What a dog is to a lamp post.

Attilla the order-taker versus St. Francis the salesperson

In any full-service restaurant or bar there are two kinds of waiters, waitresses or bartenders:

1. **Order-takers** and
2. **Service-oriented salespeople**

Which would *you* choose as your waiter? If you picked #2, good answer. If you chose number one, return to "go" and *don't* collect $200!

❖ Order-takers are to great restaurant service what a dog is to a lamp post.

❖ Order-takers are walking vending machines.

Restaurant "order-takers" treat their guests as an *interruption* of their job, rather than the *focus* of their job. Order-takers come in all shapes, sizes, genders, races, colors and religions. You can easily spot them in any restaurant by:

1. How they greet you, *("Ready to order?")*

▼   ▼   ▼   ▼

2. How they respond to a simple question like, *"What kind of beers do you have?"*

The order-taker replies by jerking a thumb in the direction of a row of multi-shaped dusty bottles on a shelf over the bar. *"They're up there,"* she says. Then she stares. And waits. She finally blurts out, *"I'll give you a few minutes!"* and darts off.

When asked if they have a wine list, the order-taker will reply *"Sure do,"* and hands you a copy. You look at it while he looks at you *and* his rapidly filling station.

● ● ● ● ● ● ● ● ● ● ● ● ●
Whose fault is it?
● ● ● ● ● ● ● ● ● ● ● ● ●

In a dining room full of order-takers the best "waiters" are the customers!

Servers aren't born "order-takers," they evolve into order-takers because it's perceived as the "path of least resistance." Order-takers usually don't understand that their behavior results in poor service and lower tips. Worst of all, they *blame the customer* for the lessened gratuities and proclaim loudly that this time, for sure, they're gonna get out and get a "real job!" But don't blame them. It's not their fault. Nobody taught them how to better serve and sell. It's the owner or manager's responsibility. (Like we said earlier, "If the son swears, strike the father.")

The good news and bad news....

The bad news is that order-taking is a *habit forming* behavior. The good news is: *so is selling.* What's the difference between the way these two servers act?

Let's contrast the behavior associated with the order-taker's "attitude" versus the salesperson's point-of-view:

AN ORDER TAKER
❖ Makes change.
❖ Is in the weeds.

- Always gets all the "cheap" customers.
- Uses *"Are you ready to order?"* as a greeting.
- Is gonna get a "real" job someday.
- When asked by our unsure guests to describe a menu item, automatically replies, *"It's good,"* to every question.
- When a guest can't make up his or her mind, grunts, *"I'll give you a few more minutes,"* and walks off.
- "Waits" on tables.
- Says, *"Do you want an appetizer?"*
- Says, *"Do you want some wine with dinner or not?"*
- Says, *"Do you want to see a dessert list?"*
- Says, *"Sorry, we're out of that."* (*"Your* move.")
- When guests hesitate at deciding on dessert, the order-taker says, *"I'll let you guys think it over."* **(Sullivan's Law refers to this as "Sellus Interruptus.")**
- Has to work doubles and pick up extra shifts because they require a high volume of guests to make up the tips they need.
- Thinks selling is pushy.
- Says, *"If my customers would've wanted it, they would've **asked** for it!"*
- Figures that the customer has a menu, let them read it and order if they want it.
- Can always tell the "cheap" customers just by looking at 'em.
- Is frightened that the customer will haunt them for the rest of their life if they suggest appetizers or wine (the "Les Miserables" complex).
- Reacts to repeated guest questions by thinking "Now what would a mad dog do in a situation like this?"
- Kicks dogs.
- Gets colds and flu from work.

A SALESPERSON
- Makes *money.*

▼   ▼   ▼   ▼

❖ Is in *control.*

❖ Makes suggestions and tips with every type of guest.

❖ Realizes that any section with customers is potentially profitable with suggestive selling.

❖ Recommends daily food and drink specials, asks questions to get a sense of what the guest is in the mood to eat or drink.

❖ Realizes that you can earn as much as you're willing to suggest. There's no "salary cap" on a salesperson's tips.

❖ Knows the ingredients, preparation procedure and price of every menu item.

❖ Recognizes a guest having difficulty making a decision and offers to help: *"What do you think you might be in the mood for ... something filling or on the lighter side?"*

❖ *Controls* the timing and pace of his or her tables and sections.

❖ Points out the appetizer list and recommends at least two different items.

❖ Says, *"We've got a great selection of wines by the glass or bottle listed here."* (Shows the guest the prices and selection.) *"I'd be happy to help you if you have any questions."*

❖ Says, *"Now we're ready for the best part of the meal ... one of our great desserts. The chocolate cheesecake is delicious and the pie of the day is deep dish apple cinnamon...."*

❖ Says, *"Sorry, we sold out of that earlier; but something similar and just as good is the...."*

❖ Knows that when guests pause at the dessert decision, this is the time to remind them that every dessert comes with two forks!

❖ Can make double the tips of an order-taker with half as many customers. Works smarter ... not harder.

❖ Knows that to suggest is to sell and to sell is to serve.

❖ Realizes that the guest may not know everything on the menu and so suggests items or "sides" that

▼   ▼   ▼   ▼

will make the meal taste better.

❖ Understands that the average menu has over 100 items to choose from and that most guests appreciate a little guidance!

❖ Takes time to "read" his or her guests by asking questions relative to their needs, then suggests only what they'd like.

❖ Knows that the *worst* that can happen is the guest says "no thanks!"

❖ Makes suggestions before the guest has to ask.

❖ Helps old ladies across the street.

❖ *Is vulnerable only to kryptonite and magic!*

Just say "NO!" to order-takers!

Whether they "mean to" or not, order-takers will eventually put even the best restaurant or bar out of business. The bottom line is that order-taking demonstrates indifference to your guests. Indifference is interpreted as bad service. And bad service is the only thing people enjoy grousing about more than the weather! But what's worth doing is worth showing someone how to do it.

Train, teach, coach and counsel

Train, teach, coach and counsel your order-takers to be salespeople *daily.* If you can't "afford" it, put off your new electronic cash register purchase for another six months and invest in something today that will pay you back $10 for every $1 you invest **(in the first two or three days!)** and it requires no new equipment whatsoever: training.

How to sell more food.

Remember, when you teach, you learn twice. Persevere. When your training stumbles, try a different way, don't abandon it. It's usually the last key on the ring that opens the lock. When your new car has a hard time starting, do you junk it and get a new one? No. It's more practical and less expensive to have it repaired. The same philosophy applies to

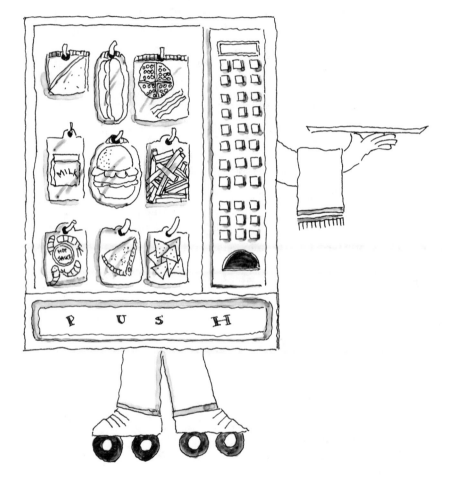

Just say "NO" to order takers

managing people and investing in daily training.

Put your money where your servers' mouths are. Teach them the right words and behavior of exemplary service and higher sales. The next four sections of *"Service That Sells!"* will help show you how.

The four steps of better service and higher sales

Enough **talk** about service and sales being synonymous. In the next four sections we'll learn *how* to raise our guest checks, improve our service, lower our costs and increase our sales and tips. We've used the following four easy steps of *Service That Sells!* to train our own waitstaff since 1982. Results? An average guest check increase of $1.03 per person **without** raising menu prices. The four steps are:

1. *See yourself as a service-oriented salesperson*
2. *Know your products*
3. *"Guide" your guests*
4. *Use the right words*

> *"Why should people go out and pay for bad service when they can stay home and get bad service for free?"*
> — *Kevin Knee*

In Pencom's award-winning *Service That Sells!* live seminar, we've trained over 100,000 restaurant, bar and hotel employees and managers in these same four steps. And while our live programs are always updated so that you rarely hear the same thing twice, these four steps are timeless and never-changing. We'd like to suggest them to you as well. Not because we think they'll work. We *know* they do.

Assign all of your waiters, waitresses, hosts, hostesses and bartenders to read this section of the book!!!

▼   ▼   ▼   ▼

Step #1 of better service and higher sales:
Think of yourself as a salesperson not an order-taker.

There are two great myths operating in the foodservice industry today. The first one is that we're in the restaurant business. As we discussed earlier, the reality is that *we're in the business of retail sales.* The other great myth is that we have waiters, waitresses and bartenders working for us. The truth is that *they are really independent contractors, commissioned sales-people.* But why should they believe that unless you can *prove* it to them?

Remember the importance of tuning in to WII-FM before you train? Here are eight reasons why a server should see him or herself as a salesperson:

● ● ● ● ● ● ● ● ● ● ● ● ● ● ● ● ● ●

"Good service can save a bad meal. A good meal cannot save bad service."
— *Doug Roth*

● ● ● ● ● ● ● ● ● ● ● ● ● ● ● ● ● ●

1. You're working for six or eight or ten hours anyway at your restaurant ... why not make the best of it? Suggest! Sell! Serve! Don't be a walking vending machine!

2. Your guests are here to buy, not browse!

3. The owner or operator pays all the expenses (food, drink, utilities, glassware, plates, napkins) advertises for all the guests and therefore takes all the risks. You make 10 percent to 20 percent on each dollar. The owner may make nothing!

4. You're tipped (10 percent to 20 percent) on a percentage of what you sell. To make more money, you can either sell more food and drinks or get tipped a higher percentage. Either way, it's based on how well you serve and sell. If you're *not* a salesperson what *are* you? A *server*? Not without selling, you're not!

▼　　▼　　▼　　▼

5. Remember, suggestive selling is not "being pushy," it's helping guests make decisions that are good for them.

6. When it's busiest, that's the time to make the most suggestions. Hunt ducks while they're flying!

7. You have everything to gain and nothing to lose! What's the absolute worst that could happen when you recommend appetizers, desserts or beverages? The guest says "no." Oh jeez. Bury me six feet under, they said "no!"

8. A salesperson easily makes more tips than an "order-taker." For example:

❖ Sell ten rum and cokes or ten vodka tonics at $2.50 each per shift, times five shifts a week, times fifty weeks a year, times 15 percent tip and you'll take home $937.50. Not bad for taking cocktail orders. ($2.50 x 10 x 5 x 50 wks. x 15 percent = $937.50!)

❖ Now upgrade those ten rum and cokes or vodka tonics to a premium rum or top shelf vodka at $3.00 each a shift, times five shifts, times fifty weeks a year, times 15 percent and you'll see $1,125 in tips! **$187.50 more just by upselling to a premium spirit**. And that's only one type of drink! ($3.00 x10 x 5 x 50 wks. x 15 percent = 1,125!)

❖ Now figure out how much more tips your servers can make in a year when they just sell an extra two appetizers or two desserts per shift. Chart it out for them. Include it in your training manuals and post it in the kitchen. See the example below.

Look at the difference

The great thing about this business is that you don't have to sell an appetizer, bottle of wine and dessert to *every* customer to make thousands more each year; only every tenth or twelfth guest. And that is easily achieved. But not if you don't try.

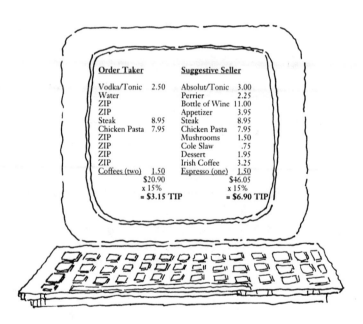

Order Taker		Suggestive Seller	
Vodka/Tonic	2.50	Absolut/Tonic	3.00
Water		Perrier	2.25
ZIP		Bottle of Wine	11.00
ZIP		Appetizer	3.95
Steak	8.95	Steak	8.95
Chicken Pasta	7.95	Chicken Pasta	7.95
ZIP		Mushrooms	1.50
ZIP		Cole Slaw	.75
ZIP		Dessert	1.95
ZIP		Irish Coffee	3.25
Coffees (two)	1.50	Espresso (one)	1.50
	$20.90		$46.05
	x 15%		x 15%
	= $3.15 TIP		= $6.90 TIP

The difference between a .250 hitter and a .300 hitter is an extra hit every *twenty* times at bat.

▼   ▼   ▼   ▼

Action Plan 1: Eight ways to increase food and beverage sales

Purging the order-taker mentality isn't easy. It involves breaking bad habits and molding new ones. As Mark Twain said, "You can't just throw a habit out the window. It must be coaxed down the stairs, one step at a time." **What you reinforce is what you get and what you don't reinforce is what you lose.** Here are eight ideas to help:

1. Give your employees a scoreboard. Start tracking sales of each server and bartender. Measure not only their *check averages* (at both lunch and dinner) but also the *number* of appetizers, sides, desserts, wine, soup, etcetera, they sell during each shift. *What gets measured gets done.*

2. Post the check averages where all the servers can see them, in order, from highest to lowest. Include each server's *"Personal Best"* highest check in parentheses next to overall average.

3. After tracking your sales, design and post bar graphs that measure the individual appetizer, dessert, wine, etcetera, sales of each server. This will make it easier to compare progress.

4. Schedule "sales" meetings at least six times a year with your entire service staff in which service and sales-oriented topics are discussed. Use these meetings as a forum to improve product knowledge, service skills and sales skills.

5. Stop referring to your staff as waiters, waitresses and bartenders, and start calling them salespeople.

6. Hold daily pre-shift team meetings in which you give *every* server and bartender specific sales and

▼   ▼   ▼   ▼

service goals for that shift. ("Frank, can you commit to selling five appetizers and at least three desserts today, and concentrate on learning three new guests' names?")

7. Follow up *during* the floor shift to make sure that each server is attempting to achieve and exceed these goals. Coach them along as you check their progress. ("Just one more dessert, Frank! You've got two tables finishing up their entrees so you've got a great opportunity here. Now what are you going to say to those guests to make that sale?")

8. HAVE FUN! Remember, he who laughs, lasts!

Step #2 of better service and higher sales:
Know your products.

Another story from Sullivan's Real-Life Casebook: I was ordering lunch at a very well known casual-theme restaurant in Phoenix. The waiter was definitely an order-taker, but a pleasant one. I could tell he was an order-taker by the guacamole on his apron, the sweat on his upper lip and the panic in the corners of his eyes. Four of his five tables had just been seated.

> *"What we have to learn to do, we learn by doing."*
> *— Aristotle*

My menu had a small clip-on note that said "Ask About Our Soup du Jour." So I asked.

"What's the soup du jour?"

My waiter was unsure. *"Just a second, sir,"* he said politely, *"I'll go find out."*

He returned momentarily, looked me in the eye and answered proudly, *"That means soup of the day, sir!"*

I paused and looked around, thinking I was on Candid Camera. Then I asked him what the soup of the day *was*. He then responded like any proud

order-taker: *"I'll go find out for you,"* and took off again! He was out of control.

My friend Paul Sollicito told me about an experience he had in a restaurant in Lancaster, Pennsylvania. He asked his waitress for a shrimp cocktail. Her deadpan response? *"I'm sorry, sir, we don't have a liquor license!"*

Hey, servers who don't know what you're selling: Get a grip. Get a clue. Get some idea. Please!

You know, we feel sorry for order-takers who don't know what they're selling: we truly do. Not only do they make less tips than they deserve but they end up walking twice as far as they have to! Order-takers also spend more time in "the weeds" than an Everglades alligator. Why? More often than not, it's because:

a. *They* waited for the *guest* to decide what's good without offering any help or suggestions.

b. They *didn't know* the answer to a customer's question.

c. They *forgot* to bring the guest an item that was supposed to go with the food in the first place.

It's easy to spot the order-takers in any restaurant; they're the ones who arrive at work full of vim and vigor and leave in a wheelbarrow, exhausted, muttering, "I'm gonna get a *real* job," to anyone within earshot. Knowing your products is the secret to Energy Conservation in the hospitality business!

▼ ▼ ▼ ▼

What will it take for me to get you in this new car today?

How important is it to know what you're selling? Picture this scenario: you're looking for a new automobile and just walked into a showroom. You're admiring the "fire engine red" sports car on display. A "salesman" walks up to you...

"Nice car, huh?" he says.

"*Really* nice," you reply. "Do you have it in any other colors besides red?"

The salesman pauses. "Uh ... I *think* so. Tell you what, you wait here and I'll go check."

"No, that's okay," you say. "Are the tires, pinstriping, floor mats, sunroof, automatic transmission and stereo standard features, or extra?"

"Good question!" he replies. "I'll go find out."

"Just a second. What kind of warranty does it come with?" you ask.

"An even better question!" the "salesman" replies. "Does it say there on the sticker? I'm not sure. I'll go find out!"

How much longer would you subject yourself to this dullard? Not very long, we'll bet. Yet how "different" sounding is the following scenario?

Guest: How's your steak sandwich here?

Server: It's good.

Guest: Hmmm ... well, how's this grilled chicken sandwich?

Server: It's good.

Guest: And the broiled salmon?

Server: It's good, too.

Guest: **(strangling the server)** How's *this* feel? *Good?!*

▼   ▼   ▼   ▼

When guests appear indecisive (which is often the case) or they ask questions like "how's the prime rib?" they're begging for some guidance or reassurance that their server can help them out a little.

Guests get very anxious when ordering, hoping they made the right choice. (If you don't believe that, why does every guest look closely at their companion's food before their own when it's delivered?)

Customers expect waitstaff and bartenders to be experts on the food and beverage your restaurant offers ... that's why **you** work there and they **don't!**

Six things to know to provide better service

Here's what every restaurant server or bartender needs to know relative to product knowledge in a restaurant or bar:

1. **The** *basic ingredients* **of each food or beverage item the restaurant sells.** "Our Chicken Monterey is six ounces of boneless grilled chicken breast rubbed with garlic and black pepper. It's smothered with red peppers, green peppers and carrots sauteed in a light artichoke cream sauce."

2. **How those ingredients are** *prepared* **and** *served.* "The chicken is grilled, the vegetables are sauteed, the artichoke sauce is ladled over the chicken. Comes with a side of wild rice."

3. **What** *"extras"* **you could suggest to go** *with* **that item.** For example, suggest a cup of soup or garden salad with any entree, grilled onions or sauteed mushrooms on a steak, cheese or fries with a burger, a bottle of chardonnay with the broiled swordfish, nachos with the margaritas, etcetera.

4. **The** *correct price* **of the item and the correct price of the "extra" or "add-on" items.**

▼ ▼ ▼ ▼

"Chicken Monterey is $8.95, cup of soup, $1.25, garden salad $1.50, side of guacamole or sour cream is only $.50."

5. **The *value* of that item.** "Best deal in town!" "Very popular," "I haven't tried it yet, but my customers love it," "Award-winning," "Plenty for one, but enough for two to share," "If you try a bottle you'll save two dollars."

6. **How choosing that item will *benefit* the guest.** "Our Irish Coffees are great! Just the thing to take the chill out of the evening!" or "Since you're each having a Bud draft, you may want to consider a pitcher. You'll save a couple dollars."

Knowing your bar products: When the guest drinks better, so do you!

Man does not live by bread alone; knowing your beverage choices is a great way to upsell premium liquor in cocktails, non-alcohol brew instead of iced tea and bottled water instead of tap water.

Let's discuss some ways that product knowledge helps us provide better beverage service.

If you serve liquor, it's critical that every server and bartender knows the beer choices, the "well" liquor brand and the "call" or premium liquor brands that they can suggest when the guest orders a drink. For example:

GUEST SAYS	SALESPERSON REPLIES
"Beer"	"Do you want a *Bud*, *Coors* or *Miller?*"
"Vodka Tonic"	"Would you like to try *Absolut* in that?"
"Rum and Coke"	"Would you like to try *Black* or *Meyers* in that?"

| "Shot of Tequila" | "Do you want to try *Cuervo* or *Cuervo 1800?*" |
| "Whiskey and water" | "How about *Jack Daniels?*" |

Practice this exercise with your staff daily using *your* particular beers or premium brands!

Why should you suggest "call" or premium liquor in every cocktail? Three reasons. First, premium liquors, generally speaking, have less impurities, so they make the drink taste better. Secondly, people are drinking less, but better. Your customers *want* premium liquor. Third, servers are tipped better on premium cocktails. So when their guests drink better, servers drink better after the shift! *(Higher Sales Tip:* Be sure to have an appetizer list available at every other seat in the bar to expedite food sales there.)

Non-alcohol beverages

We don't sell "a glass of water." We give it away. Servers receive no tip for faucet water. Teaching your waitstaff to know your non-alcohol beverage choices and then to recognize the opportunities to offer those beverages to your guests is a key to building your profit margin.

• • • • • • • • • • • • • •
We don't sell water. We give it away.
• • • • • • • • • • • • • •

Restaurateurs have a wide variety of non-alcohol brews, wines, "mocktails" and even bottled waters to offer to their guests who choose not to drink an alcohol beverage.

Print a "non-alcohol beverage" card or table tent that lists all your juices, bottled waters, coffees, sodas and non-alcohol brews or wines with their prices. Have one on each table or have every server present the list to the guest who says, "I'll have water." The perfect reply might be, *"Which would you prefer, sir, the Evian or Perrier with a twist of*

▼   ▼   ▼   ▼

lemon?" The server should then present the non-alcohol list. *"We also have a great selection of waters, juices and gourmet coffees listed here. We're featuring O'Doul's non-alcohol brew for only $2.00!"*

In these days of stagnant spirits sales, it's the smart restaurateur who educates and drills his or her staff on the product knowledge relative to non-alcohol beverages and the correct dialogue to use to sell them to your guests.

Give your staff the opportunity to upgrade an iced tea to an Arnold Palmer (half tea, half lemonade) for a quarter or fifty cents more. It's a much better tasting drink and it isn't "bottomless refills." Consider adding this beverage to your menu if you haven't already.

Don't miss the tremendous opportunity to offer the so-called "gourmet" coffees, like espresso, cappuccino, latte and special flavored or imported blends to your customers. And most importantly: don't forget to charge for the coffees or teas you do sell!

The restaurateur who trains his staff to merchandise his non-alcohol beverages instead of ignoring them will see his profits and tips rise. The restaurateur who doesn't might see his beverage sales drop as low as the period that ends this sentence.

> *"Expect people to be better than they are, it helps them to become better. But don't be disappointed when they are not, it helps them to keep trying."*
>
> *— Larry Fineberg*

The Two Laws of Product Knowledge

There are two basic rules of product knowledge and service excellence that you must never break:

Don't lie, don't lecture

1. **When in doubt, find out.** If you can't honestly answer a guest's question about a particular item, don't fake it or lie. If a guest orders a scotch and

water and you ask if they'd like to "try Jack Daniels or Jim Beam in that" you'll sound pretty silly since those are not Scotch whiskeys. Know your products. If a guest asks you what the Bearnaise Sauce tastes like and you don't know, go find out. Honesty is the best policy here. Let the guest know that you're unsure and then find out what they need to know. Remember: "It's better to ask and risk seeming foolish than to open your mouth and remove all doubt."

2. **Don't project your personal tastes on the guest.** I was at a restaurant in Dallas, Texas, that featured a Chicken Fajita Salad on the menu. I asked my waitress if the chicken was served hot or cold. She cracked her gum, looked off in the distance and sighed "*I don't know. I'm not a flesh eater!*" I felt like saying, "Well *excuuuse me!* Would you mind going back in the kitchen and asking one of the cavemen who *do* 'eat flesh' if the chicken's hot or cold????"

Now, don't get me wrong, there's nothing wrong with being a vegetarian. What's wrong was her suggesting that anyone who isn't a vegetarian has a screw loose. (And many of my strictly "leaf-eating" friends would agree!)

All I did was ask a simple, polite question that would have helped me decide what I wanted to order. She never even attempted to answer it, preferring instead to pepper me with her *opinion* instead of her *help*. Be careful of being self-righteous. For instance, if a guest asks you how the burrito is, and *you* don't like spicy food, don't automatically say "Oh, it's *really* hot." Maybe it isn't hot at all to someone who enjoys spicy Mexican food. Don't assume that your guest's tastes are identical to *yours*. Instead, you could say something like "Well, it's really popular. It's made with spicy ground beef, beans, and smothered

She's not a flesh-eater.

▼　　▼　　▼　　▼

with bubbly, melted cheese and green chili." There. You've given them an enticing mental picture of the meal without passing judgment on the guests' personal tastes. If the customer now asks if the green chili is hot, it is then appropriate to say "hotter than a French chef reading his restaurant review."

• •

Two friends walked into a bar and ordered drinks.

"I thought you were giving up the juice," said one to the other as their drinks arrived. "I was," replied the other, "but I've been suffering from insomnia."

"And a couple of drinks helps you sleep," nodded his companion.

"Actually, it doesn't help the insomnia a bit," corrected the other, "but staying up doesn't bother me the way it used to."

• •

Training tip

A great way to test and expand your staff's product knowledge (and have fun doing it) is to play a game we call *"Can You Top This?"* Pick two servers to "face off" against each other. Give each of them an appetizer, entree, dessert or specific beverage (cappuccino, wine, etcetera) as the topic. Each server can say *only one sentence at a time* and they take turns until one of the contestants can't think of a feature or benefit to say. They must use one of the following characteristics of the food or beverage each time they make a one-sentence description:

❖ **Ingredients**
"Our nachos are made with fresh pinto beans, homemade chips, cheddar and monterey jack cheese, mild jalapenos and salsa" or "Our Cadillac margarita is made with Cuervo Gold and Grand Marnier!"

❖ **Features**
"They're really popular," or "They're covered with bubbly, melted cheese," or "They're really good with spicy chicken on top," etcetera.

❖ **Benefits**
"Great to munch on while you're waiting for dinner," or "The local paper says the nachos are the best in town."

❖ **Value**
"Plenty for one but enough for two to share."

❖ **Price**
"Only $4.95; it's a great deal ... and adding spicy chicken to the nachos is only $1.25 extra."

Each server must make each statement in a way that they'd say it to a guest. The first one who is unable to respond in five seconds loses. Have your servers compete in teams. Assign a point for every right answer. Reward the winning team with a bag of candies, fruit or a well-earned round of applause. This is a great exercise to use at daily team meetings or large employee meetings.

Step #3 of better service and higher sales:
"Guide" your guests.

This is a crucial step relative to providing service and making sales. "Guiding" your guests means that servers anticipate their customers' needs by asking questions and then suggesting food or drink items that can best meet those needs. It means "leading" them through the menu, appetizers, sides, wine and desserts. **Guiding your guests is the secret to controlling your tables instead of vice versa.** Master this step and you will no longer trespass upon that unique piece of restaurant real estate known as "the weeds" *(see page 59)*.

For instance, anticipating that your guests may

▼　　▼　　▼　　▼

want to snack on something before their meal and then suggesting an appetizer to them before you leave the table to turn in their first drink order saves you time. You'll already have your guests thinking about appetizers when you return with their first drinks. Teaching your servers to guide their guests also improves the efficiency of your table seating and table turns. This means better service and more cash in their pockets.

• •

How to stay out of the weeds.

• •

There are several things your servers and host staff need to know to effectively "Guide Your Guests" and better pace and serve your customers:

❖ **Use your props**

Can you imagine Hamlet lamenting to "poor Yorick" without the skull in his hand? And where would Batman be without his utility belt? Remember, the restaurant business *is* show business and no good actor goes on "stage" without using props. "Props" are wine lists, menus or table tents that you can use to point out specific juices, appetizers, "sides", beers, wine or desserts to your guests. It's a great way to initiate a suggestion for a particular item. Fast food operations feature full-color pictures of menu items on their reader boards. These are great props to point out to customers who are trying to make a decision. Many restaurants include appetizers or specialty drink lists on each table. These can be great sales props in addition to the menu. If you use a specialty drink table tent or appetizer list, always open the list and *hand it to the guest* when recommending an item.

Drinks or food themselves can be

great sales props, too. A sizzling platter of fajitas or a mouth-watering dessert gets customers hungry for a similar treat. A tall, frosty Piña Colada made with a dark rum is an extremely eye-appealing drink. Let the other customers in your section see the drink as you deliver it. Many customers will say, *"I want one of those!"*

❖ **Recognize your opportunities**
In order to "guide" your guests into trying something they'll enjoy, you must first identify the six opportunities you have to suggestively sell!

Opportunity #1. The Initial Greeting and Beverage Zone

> *What to suggest first:* Juice, coffee, cocktails, beer, wine, soda, etcetera. (Remember, every cocktail order should be followed by a suggestion to upgrade that drink to a premium liquor!) "Can I get you something to drink? A glass of wine, a beer or a cocktail? We've got a great selection of specialty drinks and beers listed here."

> *What to suggest before you leave the table:* Appetizers and perhaps point out daily specials.

Opportunity #2. The Appetizer Zone

> *What to suggest first:* A choice of at least two appetizers, cups of soup or "starter" salads.

> *What to suggest before you leave:* Extras on the appetizers (for example: Nachos Deluxe instead of plain nachos, chicken on the potato skins, etcetera), daily specials, entrees.

SPECIAL
TODAY
ENTRÉE
RED FLORIDA SNAPPER
PASTA
TORTELLINI PRIMAVERA
APPETIZER
BLACK BEAN SOUP

▼ ▼ ▼ ▼

● ● ● ● ● ● ● ● ● ● ●
Suggest deluxe,
settle for plain.
● ● ● ● ● ● ● ● ● ● ●

Opportunity #3. The Entree Zone

What to suggest first: Daily specials or entrees. Take the order.

What to suggest before you leave: "Extras," or "sides" to compliment the entree.

Opportunity #4. The "Extras" or "Sides" Zone

What to suggest first: Cheese or fries with the burger, cup of soup, garden salad (if missed during the appetizer zone), sides of onion rings, mushrooms, bacon, vegetable du jour, guacamole, sour cream, lettuce, tomato, chips or any or all of the above.

What to suggest before you leave: That the guest *saves room* for one of your great desserts, (recommend at least two by name).

Opportunity #5. The Wine Zone

Note: The period between soup or salad and entree is the longest delay diners face and the perfect time to suggest wine. Wine should also be suggested in the "Initial Greeting."

What to suggest first: Wine by the bottle, split or glass. Ask the guest what their preferences are. Try these three simple questions:

1. "Have you had a chance to look over our wine list?"
2. "Do you prefer red or white wine?"
3. "Do you like a sweet or drier wine?" These three simple questions allow you (in less than 30 seconds) to find out what kind of wine your guests prefer and which one to suggest. That way the guest feels like **they** made the decision when actually **you** helped make it for them.

▼ ▼ ▼ ▼

What to suggest as you pour the remainder of their first bottle into their glasses: "Can I bring you a second bottle of wine now, or would you like to wait a few minutes?"

● ● ● ● ● ● ● ● ● ● ● ● ● ● ● ●

How to sell more wine.

● ● ● ● ● ● ● ● ● ● ● ● ● ● ● ●

Opportunity #6. The Dessert Zone

What to suggest first: Desserts, cordials, liqueurs, specialty drinks, cappuccino, espresso, coffee or tea.

What to recommend: A cup of coffee or tea with every dessert and, of course, a return visit!

Now that you know your six opportunities to sell, let's return to another helpful hint for guiding your guests.

Know how to determine what your guests are "in the mood" for

How? By asking questions:

❖ *"Can I get you something to drink? A glass of fresh orange juice, a cup of coffee or tea?"*

❖ *"Are you real hungry or would you prefer something lighter?"*

❖ *"Have you had a chance to look over our wine list?"*

❖ *"Do you know what you'd like to order? I'd be happy to help you if you have any questions. The blueberry pancakes look great today."*

▼   ▼   ▼   ▼

Selling out of sequence: don't give up the ship

You can always suggest food or beverage "out of sequence" to make the sale. For instance, if your guests at lunch are in a hurry, take their order, turn it in and then go back to the table with the appetizer suggestion. "I just turned in your lunch orders, folks. They'll be ready in about 10 minutes. Can I get you a cup of soup or some guacamole and chips to munch on while you're waiting?"

If you're waiting on a group of drinkers and suggest appetizers to them, but they decline, be sure to suggest appetizers again after the third round. Alcohol stimulates hunger.

At dinner, you may take the entree order, turn it in and realize you missed an opportunity to suggest wine. **It's okay** to go back to the table with the wine list and say, *"I've turned in your entree orders and I thought you might be interested in looking over our wine list...."* The key here is to search for and create opportunities to suggest and sell. They say that "opportunity knocks," but the truth is, sometimes it just "goes without saying!" Don't give up the ship ... you may have to navigate through that swamp ahead!

• • • • • • • • • • • •

Think backwards.

• • • • • • • • • • • •

How guiding your guests helps you eat your "weedies"

It starts slowly. Unassuming. Quietly. Then, "The Rush" comes. And suddenly, no one is safe. Not your calmest manager or your newest waitress. It can even turn the most disciplined mind into a Freudian smorgasbord, the lithest body into jello, the most composed server into the "Swamp Thing." It sometimes transforms the most seasoned salesperson into a walking vending machine. It can give a previously calm server the appearance of a chained monkey in the middle of a metal detector. It slices deep into waitstaff morale and cuts deeper into restaurant profits. It increases blood pressure, tempers, stress and turnover. It shrinks tips and swells feet. Who does it hurt? Guests. Servers. Managers. Trainers. Everybody. What is it?

It's called *"The Weeds"* (or being "swamped") and it's a phenomenon found in every restaurant and bar and it's every servers' favorite nightmare. But unlike most nightmares this one happens for real. Every day. In every restaurant, in every bar, and in every town, servers suddenly lose control of their station or bar. It's a terrible state to be in. We know, cuz we've been there, too!

We all know how helpless-feeling and service-affecting "in the weeds" can be. What we don't usually realize is that our servers do have the ability to control their sections instead of their sections controlling them. How? **It starts by making sure all assigned sidework is completed to par levels before the shift begins.** Prepping beyond par levels is always recommended, especially napkins and silverware roll-ups!

The next step is to ensure that systems and procedures facilitate service and sales instead of creating obstacles to them. For instance, many restaurateurs buy computerized ordering systems to speed up food preparation and billing. But how is customer service affected when the waiter has to stand in line to gain access to the single terminal in the kitchen instead of being on the floor helping to pamper his guests?

You can run but you can't hide.

Sidework must be completed, and systems must support service delivery (not vice versa) before control can be established and service and sales delivered.

▼　　▼　　▼　　▼

"I don't have time to sell."

Most servers wrongly believe that once they're swamped they haven't got *time* to make sales because they're "too busy." It's the manager's responsibility to show them that just the opposite is true. Guiding the guest is the key to staying **in** the money and **out** of the weeds. *Making suggestions* is the server's verbal "weed-eater." Your waitstaff must be taught how to take *control* instead of Pepto-Bismol! How do we teach them to properly guide their guests? By learning to do four things:

• • • • • • • • • • • • • • • • • • •

How do you keep customers from bugging you?

• • • • • • • • • • • • • • • • • • •

♦ **Observe**
♦ **Anticipate**
♦ **Prioritize**
♦ **Act**

Guide those guests! It's a simple answer to the restaurant servers' oldest question: **how do you keep those "dang customers" from interrupting you so you can do your job?** The solution is as simple as the cattails in your servers' aprons: suggesting appetizers, specials, wine and desserts to your guests *before* they have to ask *if* you have any of the above. Here's a detailed explanation of the four steps that can make you a "Professional Foodservice Weed-Eater."

Observe

Before you enter the dining room, take a few seconds to quickly *observe* your section or station. Scan the faces of your guests and the tabletops in front of them. Assess where you're at, what you and your guests will need next and which table you'll have to get to first, second, third, etcetera.

Anticipate

When your servers approach a newly-seated table, they should *anticipate* their guests needs by saying, *"Can I get you something to drink from the bar? A glass of wine, a beer, a cocktail or maybe one of our great specialty drinks listed here."* (She points out the drinks on the menu.) *"We have Gold Margaritas on special today for only $3.50."* Elapsed time: 8 seconds. The guest now has an "overview" of the beverage selections (wine, beer, cocktails, specialty drinks) and the daily drink special (Gold Margaritas for $3.50). The server has helped guide the guest to a quicker decision. Compare *that* dialogue to this exchange:

Server: "Are you ready to order?"
Guest 1: "Do you have wines by the glass?"
Server: (looks at table being seated next to her) "Uh. Yes we do."
Guest 2: "I don't know ... hmmm ... maybe a margarita...."
Server: (bead of sweat forms on her forehead as two of her other tables are seated) "How 'bout I give you a few minutes to...."

• • • • • • • • • • • • • • • • • • •
Work smarter, not harder.
• • • • • • • • • • • • • • • • • • •

Guest 1: (notices drink list) "Are these your specialty drinks?"
Server: "Yes. (Forced smile ala Mona Lisa) How 'bout I just...."
Guest 1: Which are good?
Guest 2: "Does that say 'Gold Margarita' on the special board there?"
Guest 1: "Oh, I know! What kinds of beers do you have?"
Server: "ARGHHH!"

Elapsed time: 2 minutes. This server is so close to the swamp that she could order an alligator sandwich. (And make it snappy!) Teach your servers to always observe their station, then anticipate their guests' needs and make suggestions before they have to ask. It gives the server more time and more control. Better tips, too!

Prioritize

The next step for servers (and managers) to effectively guide their guests is to *prioritize* the needs of everyone in your section. Which of the tables needs your attention first? Who's second? Third?

In general, the following four diners should always warrant your servers' primary attention, though not necessarily in this order. Every restaurant has different policies and procedures but the following guidelines can help your servers mentally prioritize their responsibilities:

Newly-seated guests

Always acknowledge the newest customers in your section *first*. After all, those guests are probably anxious and most certainly unoccupied. Remember Sullivan's Law: **Unoccupied time passes slower than occupied time.** It only takes a moment to smile and say, "I'll be right with you!" This will reduce the guests' anxieties and they'll begin to relax. Don't turn your guests into "waiters."

• • • • • • • • • • • •
Sullivan's Law
• • • • • • • • • • • •

Guests who have a problem with their food or drink

These guests are always a server's priority. Handle food or drink mistakes immediately. Take it back to the kitchen or bar as soon as the guest complains; don't check with all your other tables first, carrying the "problem" food or drink on your tray. The guest with the problem expects and deserves a quick solution. They don't want to see you take your time while they wait.

Guests who just received food

Watch the look on your guests' faces as they first taste their food or beverage. Then always try to check with your guests before they've had *two bites* of their meal. Why? If there's a mistake you can handle it before it becomes a *problem.* This opportunity gives you a chance to find out if the food is good and you can also see if they need anything else like ketchup, mayonaise, napkins, etcetera.

••••••••••••••••••••

The two-bite checkback.

••••••••••••••••••••

Guests who are ready to pay

People may relax at a restaurant or bar table for hours, but when they're ready to leave, they're in a hurry to go. When guests are ready to pay, *process their check quickly.* And more importantly, **reconcile the tab and get their change back even more quickly.** After all, this is the time they're thinking "TIP." Help them leave as quickly as they need to — but only when they're *ready* to go.

Point out to your servers that it only takes a few seconds to stand apart from their section and **visually scan each table.** Have them get in the habit of asking:

❖ What stage of dining are my guests involved in? What do they need now?

❖ What stage are they approaching? What will they need at that point?

❖ Which of my tables have just **been** seated?

❖ Just received food?

❖ Ready to pay?

❖ Potentially having a problem with their food or drink?

❖ The key here is simple: **Plan your work, then work your plan.**

▼   ▼   ▼   ▼

Now . . . ACT!

The fourth step in helping your servers control their sections and improve their service and sales is to teach them how to ACT, not just re-act. This means that once they *observe* and then *anticipate* the dining stage each of their tables is approaching, followed by mentally Prioritizing the tables that need their attention first, your servers must then *act* to take care of those guests' needs immediately. This is precisely the point at which most servers either remain on terra firma or move toward the quicksand. This is the town limit sign of "The Weeds." Many servers observe their full station, anticipate their guests' needs, prioritize their tables and then fail to **act**, which is the most important step in the entire process. Remember the old cartoon: "Ready? Fire! Aim!" Ready? Set? Go. Act. Servers, don't "wait" on your section, **control it**. Serve, suggest, sell. Don't fall victim to the myth that once your station or section is full, now you're "too busy" to suggest appetizers, sides, wines or desserts. That's backwards logic. Your stations are *full*, brimming with opportunity (and potential tips!) so "make hay while the sun shines." **Suggestive selling is the key to being in the money and out of the weeds.** (Almost as important is teaching your servers to pre-bus tables as they work their section. *No one goes into the kitchen or out to the dining room empty-handed!* The server who takes control of his or her station makes good money and stays energetic. The "Swamp Thing" gives poor service, has swollen feet and warns us all that someday he or she will be getting a "real" job.

Hey, working in this business puts food on our family's table, clothes on our backs and pays our bills. What could be more "real" than that?

- - - - - - - - - - - - - - - - - - -

"Man who says it cannot be done should not interrupt man doing it."

— Sam Wo

- - - - - - - - - - - - - - - - - - -

Action plan 2: How to teach your servers to "guide" their guests

1. Assign this section of the book to all of your servers to read.

2. Call a 90-minute staff meeting. Servers, bartenders and managers should attend.

3. On a flip chart, list the "Six Opportunities to Sell" discussed in this chapter.

4. As a group, discuss and list the specific items in your restaurant or bar that your servers could suggest to your guests in each of the six areas.

5. The meeting facilitator should then discuss and demonstrate all of the sales "props" we can use to help sell (menus, table tents, wine lists, specialty drink or appetizer lists.)

6. A table should be set up in the front of the room. The facilitator should demonstrate the wrong way and then the right way to serve and sell in each of the Six Opportunities (initial greeting, appetizers, entrees, extras, wine and desserts).

7. Now choose two managers to play the guests. Pick six different servers to come up and role play the correct dialogue, product knowledge and use of props. Have each role-player demonstrate one of the Six Opportunities to Sell.

8. Ask your staff to list all the things that can make a server lose control in their section (i.e. not doing sidework, not enough roll-ups, running out of ice, etcetera) and then brainstorm the solutions. Discuss how to use the "Observe, Anticipate, Prioritize, Act" model to control a four-table section at different stages of dining. Draw a four-table station on a flip chart and map out the prioritized steps necessary to most efficiently serve that section.

▼   ▼   ▼   ▼

Step #4 of better service and higher sales:
Use the right words.

All of us learned a long time ago that there are "right" words and "wrong" words to use when we ask for things. For instance:

> **Wrong:** "Gimme that!" (Slap from Mom.)
> **Right:** "Please pass the pie." (Smile from Mom.)

In the hospitality business too, there are wrong and right words and phrases to use when serving our customers. There are words and phrases that make our guests comfortable and there are words that make them feel like they're bothering you by taking up space at your counter, table or bar. Let's discuss phraseology in a way that won't require a pocket dictionary or thesaurus.

Here's a list of "wrong" questions that we'd like to suggest your staff *never* uses:

"Kelp you?" (Never be abrupt or snappy.)

"Just one for dinner?" (Don't offend single patrons. Solo diners are some of our best customers.)

"Ready to order, honey?" (Sure, darling.)

"Whatta ya need, pal?" (Not a wiseguy for a bartender!)

"You don't want any wine with dinner, do you?" (Why would I want anything to make my meal taste better?)

"Do you want some dessert?" (Don't bother to tell me what you have.)

"Ya want something to drink?" (Probably. What do you have?)

"Do you want an appetizer?" (Is there a choice or selection?)

"Is everything okay?" (Yeah. Is "okay" your standard?)

"Alright, let's start with you, okay?" (Don't *start* with me, pal.)

"Your table's ready, wanna follow me?" (Are you in a hurry?)

● ● ● ● ● ● ● ● ● ● ● ● ● ● ● ● ● ●
Use open-ended questions.
● ● ● ● ● ● ● ● ● ● ● ● ● ● ● ● ● ●

"Do you want another?" (Do you remember what it was?)

"What was that you're drinking?" (I didn't think so.)

Teach servers to be *diners* first and waitstaff second. They should always try to serve from the *guest's* point-of-view. Questions like the ones above only serve the person asking the question, *not* the guest. Take your time with every guest, acknowledge them with a warm smile, make eye contact and talk to them, not at them. Not only do the questions above reflect service indifference, they also limit sales opportunities. At your next staff meeting, a fun exercise to use is asking your servers to list and discuss all the questions *they* hate to hear when dining out. The next section of *Service That Sells!* looks at the right words relative to menu merchandising.

Use Descriptive Adjectives

If you want your guests to drink wine, for instance, *don't* say: *"Want some wine with dinner?"* This

▼   ▼   ▼   ▼

question forces the guest to answer with a "yes" or "no" right there, and most probably the answer is "no" since you haven't made it sound appealing enough, offered choices or asked them *their* preferences.

●●●●●●●●●●●●●●●●●●●●●●●

What you say is what they'll get.

●●●●●●●●●●●●●●●●●●●●●●●

Listen to the difference when we use words that leave the question open: *"Have you had a chance to look over our wine list? We've got a great selection and some very good values. The Sutter Home White Zinfandel and the Soleo are very popular."* Now the guest is enticed to ask *you* more questions about your wine list! (See appendix for 43 more ways to sell wine.)

Since you can't bring *every* dish or drink out to the guest to show them what it looks like, it's important that you're able to describe each item in a way that creates a mental picture in the guest's mind.

For instance, you could describe a dish called Seafood Gumbo Casserole in the following manner:

"It's seafood in a gumbo baked in a casserole. Lotta people order it."

Read that description out loud. Sound tempting? We don't think so, either. Now look at — and listen to — the difference a few "descriptive adjectives" can make:

"The seafood gumbo casserole? It's really popular. It's four ounces of Florida *stone crab*, and fresh *bay scallops*, sauteed in *white wine* with snow *peas*, mild *peppers*, and basil-garlic *cream sauce*. It comes with a garden salad for only $10.95!"

Read *that* description aloud. Can't you hear (and practically see) the difference?

Using the right words can make even the most routine beverage sound more appealing to purchase. For instance:

Guest: Do you have beer on tap?
Order-Taker: Yeah. Bud or Coors, dollar-seventy-five.

▼ ▼ ▼ ▼

Now listen to the difference:

Guest: Do you have beer on tap?
Salesperson: You bet. Bud Light, Coors, or Miller in a giant 14 ounce frosty mug for only a dollar-seventy-five.

Creating "mental pictures" in your guests' minds does not mean that you need "psychic" powers or a cook named Kreskin to merchandise your menu. Listed on the next page are 85 words and phrases you can use to make your food and beverage sound more appealing to your guests. (What you say is what they'll get!)

▼   ▼   ▼   ▼

Swami Sullivan's Guide to "CREATING MENTAL PICTURES" (Or words that help sell!)

FOOD

Lightly breaded
Overflowing
Really popular
Spicy-not hot
Heaping
Dip and eat
Piping hot
Unique
Top choice
Sauteed
Seared
Properly aged
Honey baked
Char-broiled
Natural
New
Original recipe
Favorite
Poached
Plenty for one, but....
    enough to share
Our guests love it
Steamed in beer
One of a kind taste
So fresh it slept in
    the ocean last night.
Homemade
Incredible
Sprinkled
Crisp
Legendary
Radi-cool

Stuffed
Bubbly, melted cheese
Fun to share
Fresh daily
Extra size
Super size
Fresh
Award-winning
Center Cut
Jumbo Stuffed
Golden brown
Marinated
Jet fresh
Garden-fresh
Chilled
Famous
Original
Savory
Broasted
Be sure to save
    room for....
Traditional recipe
Brushed in lemon
Two handed
Sold out, not
    "ran out"
Frosty
To die for
Creamy
Tangy
Crunchy

BEER

Ice cold	Frosty mug
Smooth	Lighter
Crisp	Special
Featured	Popular

DRINKS

Fresh fruit	Special
Frozen	Tropical
Hand mixed	Creamy
Famous	Giant
Fresh-squeezed	

• • • • • • • • • • • • •
Words that increase
beverage sales.
• • • • • • • • • • • • •

WINE

Dry	Full bodied
Vintage	Robust
Mellow	Semi-dry
Elegant	Fruity
Imported	

Now that we know some words that help sell, let's discuss the concept of primacy and recency or....

People remember the first and last thing you say....

It's a fact. In our popular *Service That Sells!* seminars we do an exercise with the audience that proves this point, and you can use it with your staff as well.

Read off a random list of sixteen numbers. Announce that you'll pay ten dollars cash to anyone who can remember those numbers (without writing them down) in the exact sequence you read them. No one will. Now, ask if anyone can remember the *first* and *last* numbers. Most of the audience will.

The point is that servers will increase the odds of a guest buying a particular food or drink item if the server mentions it *twice*, once at the beginning of their greeting and again at the end.

For instance, if you want to increase your wine sales, teach your servers to greet guests with this statement:

"Hello, can I get you something to drink from the bar? A glass of wine, a beer or a cocktail? Our featured wine tonight is a Sutter Home Cabernet."

Notice how we mentioned wine in general first, then a *specific* wine last? This gives the guest a subtle psychological "tug" to consider our suggestions.

If you want to sell more beer, train your servers to say, *"Can I get you something to drink? A beer, a glass of wine or a cocktail? We've got a great selection of bottled beers listed here* (use your prop!) *and Michelob on tap!"*

Teach your staff to use this initial beverage greeting with *every* guest. Substitute whatever beverage *you* want to sell as the first and last drink you mention. You'll be amazed at how well it works. After teaching this method to our 400-plus servers we saw wine-by-the-glass sales increase 15 percent and specialty drink sales soar 21 percent!

• • • • • • • • • • • • • • •

Nine ways to sell more food and drink.

• • • • • • • • • • • • • • •

Let's look at nine ways that waiters, waitresses, and bartenders can improve service and increase tips by using the right words (and the right behavior).

1. Use the "right words" to sell beverages

Use this dialogue when first greeting guests who have just been seated: *"Can I get you something to drink?* (Pause) ... *A* **beer, a glass of wine,** *a cocktail or maybe one of our* **great specialty drinks** (hand guest the drink list) ... *we have a great list here. We also have a special on Bud Light today, only $2.50, and our featured wine special is Sutter Home Chardonnay for $3.25 a glass."*

Analysis: This dialogue saves you time by:

- ❖ Giving the guest an "overview" of all the drink options available (wine by the glass, beer by the glass, bottle or pitcher, and cocktail or specialty drinks).

- ❖ Making suggestions *before* the guest has to ask (*"Excuse me, do you have Michelob?"*).

- ❖ Allowing the server to point out *all* the drink options (including daily specials) in a total elapsed time of *less than 15 seconds!* Now that's saving time!

- ◆ For ten ways to SELL MORE BEER see the appendix in back.

REMEMBER: Use your "props" to help reinforce the dialogue. Always *hand* the appetizer list to your guests to review while you leave to get their first drinks. Suggest a choice of your two favorite appetizers (or two you think your guests would enjoy) *before* you leave the table.

• • • • • • • • • • •
Never say, "Do you want ... ?"
• • • • • • • • • • •

2. Use the "right words" to sell appetizers
Use this dialogue after delivering the first drinks to your guests (and after pointing out the appetizer list): ***"Which one of our appetizers looks good to you today?"***

Analysis:

- ❖ Never say, *"Do you want an appetizer?"* Assume the sale! Ask *which* appetizer they'd prefer.
- ❖ After asking the question above ("Which appetizer looks good today?"), be ready to suggest a choice of different appetizers. For instance, don't suggest two deep-fried appetizers. Suggest a contrast, such as potato skins or a cup of soup.

▼   ▼   ▼   ▼

    ❖ If your guests appear to have limited time, like at lunch, suggest "quick" appetizers, such as breadsticks, guacamole and chips, a garden salad, or a cup of soup, etcetera.
    ❖ Always have appetizer lists in front of each stool at the bar.
    ❖ Suggesting appetizers before the customer has to ask you about them *saves you time!*

    ◆ For ten ways to Sell More Appetizers, see appendix in back.

REMEMBER: ALWAYS suggest appetizers. People love 'em! And don't forget, it's never too late to suggest appetizers; even after you take and process the entree order, you can always return to the table and recommend an appetizer that can be served quickly. Appetizers give your guests something to do while waiting for the entree. It helps eliminate the feeling of "waiting."

3. Use the "right words" to sell wine
(Don't be a "Cork-Dork!")
There are five opportunities to suggest wine in a typical dining situation at a full service restaurant:

The five times to suggest wine.

1. In your initial greeting.
2. When you take the entree order.
3. Right after turning in the entree order.
4. In the period between soup or salad and serving the main course.
5. After dinner. Always suggest dessert wines such as port, cabernet or a glass of champagne.

Use the following dialogue to initiate wine sales.
"Have you decided on a wine to go with your lunch/ dinner today?" (Hand the guest the wine list.) *"We've got a great selection by the glass, split or bottle listed here."*

(Pause, wait for response.) *"Do you prefer red or white?"*
If the guest replies *"white,"* then ask *"do you prefer a
sweeter or drier white wine?"* This steers the guest into
making a decision they want to make.

Analysis:

❖ Suggesting wine before the guest has to ask
saves time.

❖ Wine sales generate the *biggest tips* for the
server.

Hot Tip: Selling the *second* bottle of wine to the
guests who have just finished the first one is easy if
you say: *"Can I bring you another bottle now
or when I bring your entrees?"* as you pour
out the remainder of their first bottle into
their glasses. Ask your local wine rep to set
up wine training and tasting seminars for
your staff. Pair up your wines with your
food and appetizers.

◆ See appendix for 45 ways to sell
wine

4. **Use the right words to sell more desserts**
(Remember, desserts are the fifth food group!)
Always suggest desserts at least twice: once after
taking the entree order (*"Be sure to save room for
our homemade hot pecan pie!"*), and then again after
clearing the entree plates. Don't*ever* say, *"Do you
want some dessert?"* That doesn't sound enticing.
Make it sound irresistible. Try this format:

> *"Now we're ready for the best part of the meal, one
> of our great desserts! Maybe the Mud Pie made
> with chocolate chip ice cream, oreo cookie crust and
> covered with a Kahlua-chocolate fudge sauce?
> Our homemade pie today is fresh peach, and it's
> great topped with cinnamon ice cream."*

◆ See appendix for 10 more ways to sell dessert

▼ ▼ ▼ ▼

Hot Tips:

- Always suggest dessert before you suggest coffee. To many people, offering coffee signals the end of the meal.
- Always suggest a range of two *different* types of dessert, such as a chocolate one and a fruit one.
- Suggest cappuccino, espresso, liqueurs or dessert wine first to go with the dessert your guests order. If they decline, then suggest coffee.
- Suggest that your guests split a dessert if they indicate that they're "too full." (*All of our desserts come with two forks!*")

5. Use the "Sullivan Head Nod"

There is another tool we use for *Service that Sells*, and it could be the most effective one of all when combined with the "right words." We call this tool the "Sullivan Nod." Quite simply, this means that the server or bartender very slowly nods their head *up and down* as they make the food or beverage suggestion to the guest. It never ceases to amaze us how the guest almost always agrees to the suggestion when it's accompanied by this discreet body language!

If you use nothing else in this book, use this!

Some examples:

Guest:	...and a Pepsi, please.
Server:	Large? (nod)
Guest:	Yeah, large.

Guest:	I'll have a beer.
Server:	Would you like to try (slow head nod and smile) a Miller Lite or Bud Dry?
Guest:	Uh, yeah. Bud Dry please.

Guest:	I'll have a piece of that blueberry pie.
Server:	Would you like a scoop of (slow head

nod) French Vanilla ice cream on that?

Guest: Umm, yeah. Why not? Thanks!

Guest: I'll have the New York Strip. Medium-rare.

Server: Good choice. Can I bring you a bowl of our French Onion soup (slow head nod) or homemade vegetable soup to start?

Guest: Yeah, French Onion soup sounds good.

*Try the "Nod." You won't **believe** how well it works.*

6. Customers are people, too!

A lot of servers are unsure how to initiate or begin their "sales" presentation with guests. One of the best approaches we've heard was from a waitress in Memphis, Tennessee. She offers the menus to her guests, smiles, makes some small talk and then asks: *"Would you care for a couple of recommendations?"* "Read" your customers. Always engage them in conversation first to establish rapport. Talk to them about the weather, compliment them on their clothing, ask them what they do. It is said that people don't care what you know until they know that you care. Remember the four steps we listed on page 27: *"Look at me. Smile at me. Talk to me. Thank me."*

• • • • • • • • • • • • • • • • •
Use the weather to sell.
• • • • • • • • • • • • • • • • •

7. Use "try" to buy

When suggesting sides or extras or recommending premium liquor in cocktails use the word "try" when mentioning the upgrade. That way the guest knows that it will cost a little more, but will make the drink taste much better. For example:

Guest: We'll have the large garlic chicken pizza.

Server:	Would you like to try (*Sullivan nod*) some cheese breadsticks with that?
Guest:	Sure!

Guest:	I'll have the large burrito with chicken.
Server:	Very good, sir. Would you like to try a side of sour cream with that?
Guest:	Sounds good to me.

8. Double "features"

Another great word to use when describing alcohol beverages (or even appetizers and desserts) is "feature." For example, "Our California Reserve is our *featured* wine-by-the-glass this evening," or "we're *featuring* Cape Codders tonight for only $2.50." Some servers we know use the word "featured" when recommending their favorite beverage or dessert even if it's not offered at a discounted price. The word "featured" sounds special and value-oriented.

9. Always suggest a choice

One of the key elements of using the right words is to always offer a choice of at least two different items when suggesting food or beverage. Why? Well, some guests may not like the type of food or brand item you're suggesting if you only mention one.

Don't put all your eggs in one basket.

For example, *don't* say:

Guest:	I'll have a vodka martini, rocks, twist.
Server:	Do you want to try Kamchatka vodka in that?
Guest:	Uh, no thanks. (He's an Absolut drinker.)

Many vodka drinkers (or any premium liquor drinkers) are very particular about the brand they prefer. Offer a choice of at least two different vodkas instead. Offering a choice usually results in the guest "calling back" for the upsell if you didn't mention "their" brand:

> **Guest:** I'll have a scotch rocks, please.
> **Server:** Would you like to try Dewar's, Cutty or Johny Walker Red in that?
> **Guest:** Umm, do you have J&B scotch?
> **Server:** Yes sir, we sure do.
> **Guest:** I'll have that, thanks!

If you're suggesting appetizers or desserts, recommend two that are very different from each other to give the guest an idea of the "range" of appetizers you offer. For example:

"We've got a great selection of appetizers listed here (point them out on the menu). The potato skins and the fresh vegetable dip platter are both very popular."

"Practice doesn't make perfect. Perfect practice makes perfect."

Vince Lombardi

▼   ▼   ▼   ▼

Don't ever say, "Do you want some nachos?" What if they hate nachos but love the crab dip you *didn't* suggest?

These nine steps are key characteristics of an effective service-oriented sales person. We'd like to suggest that managers role-play these steps with their servers until they're proficient at each one.

COURSE 3: Where's the hidden treasure in your restaurant? summary

Assign this section of the book for your waitstaff and managers to read. Quiz them on the contents. Add a dollar sign to the left of your annual customer count. Now use the following steps to teach your servers how to raise your guest checks one dollar.

1. Teach your servers to see themselves as salespeople, not order-takers.

- Salespeople make better tips.

- Salespeople provide better service.

- When the restaurant succeeds, employees succeed.

2. Teach your service staff to know your products.

- Knowing what you're selling allows you to sell more.

- Knowing not only what is in it, but what would go good with it.

- Test product knowledge daily at team meetings with "Can You Top This?" on page 52.

3. Guide your guests.

 ◆ Make suggestions before they have to ask.

 ◆ Use your props to help sell.

 ◆ Control your station instead of vice versa: (observe, anticipate, prioritize, act).

 ◆ Train your waitstaff to recognize the six opportunities to serve and sell:

   1. Initial Greeting and Beverage zone
   2. Appetizer zone
   3. Entree zone
   4. Extras or "Sides" zone
   5. Wine zone
   6. Dessert zone

4. Use the right words.

 ◆ Use descriptive adjectives to create mental pictures.

 ◆ Ask open-ended questions to get guests buying instead of just replying.

 ◆ Use the "Sullivan Nod" when making suggestions to create agreement in your guests.

 ◆ Use the word "try" when recommending a premium liquor in a cocktail.

 ◆ Always offer a choice of at least two items when making suggestions.

5. Role play the four steps with your servers until they can do it in their sleep. Don't leave anything out. Coach them every shift, every week, every month.

COURSE 4: Desserts
"Watch your waste"

How to control costs in your restaurant or bar

Now that we know how to improve our service, raise our guest checks one dollar per person and find the "hidden treasure" in our restaurants and bars, you're probably saying to yourself, "Nice! Glad I read this book! Suddenly, our morale is great, the turnover's zero and my sales are soaring!"

Yeah. Right.

Soar your sales all you want, but let's first do a dose of "hospitality reality," shall we? There's another facet of profitability that must be managed at

• •

"Ever run out of month at the end of your money?"

— Tom Hopkins

• •

least as well as, if not better than, your sales and service skills. We're talking about waste watching and cost control. Cutting costs is a wonderful thing. It's what separates private industry from the government.

If you increase sales, you naturally increase costs. More food, beverage and dry goods must be purchased, stored or prepared. If you **don't** teach your staff to sell, you're increasing the likelihood of more wasted food and beverage, higher overall costs, lower profit margin and possibly a "going out of business" sale! The beauty of suggestive selling is that if you teach your staff how to get better at merchandising your menu, gross sales will increase exponentially to offset the wholesale cost of the additional food and beverage you're selling while your labor costs simultaneously **decrease**. (Your cooks are still

▼ ▼ ▼ ▼

on the clock whether they're making two appetizers or twenty appetizers per hour.)

However, if you increase sales 8 percent and simultaneously raise costs 10 percent you can't come out ahead. But learn how to increase sales 5 percent and simultaneously lower costs by 2 percent and suddenly you're making Big Bucks in the hospitality industry!

To be successful, you must minimize the costs and maximize the yield of:

❖ The food and beverage you're buying (and hopefully *selling)*.

❖ The service accessories or dry goods you're providing and hopefully maintaining (tables, glasses, napkins, flatware, silverware, etcetera).

❖ The business necessities you're procuring (insurance, taxes, utilities, accounting, payroll, bookkeeping, etcetera).

• •

"Running a business these days is like Dudley Moore dancing with Raquel Welch. The overhead is fantastic."

— *Steve Yeager*

• •

Why do restaurants go out of business? Not because of bad service or poor management; the bottom line is **that they couldn't cover their costs.**

There isn't enough room in this book for a detailed discussion of Profitability Management 101. But we do have some realistic ideas that have worked for us and many of our colleagues and clients to lower costs in your restaurant or bar immediately.

It all begins by getting everyone who works in your restaurant to join "Waste Watchers." And not "anonymously!"

A Toast to the Heart-of-the-House

It's impossible to discuss cost control without also discussing the most critical part of any restaurant operation: the kitchen. These hard-working, butt-busting and fun-loving crew members are arguably the most important department of any successful restaurant operation. And we salute them. Thought: refer to your kitchen crew as the "Heart-of-the-House," not the "back" of the house (an idea from Denise Minchella) it sounds nicer. And

A waiter quit his job to become a traffic cop and said: "The pay and the hours aren't great, but at least the customer is always wrong!"

let's face it, service isn't just what the server gives, it's what the prep cook gives, or dishwasher gives, or chef gives so that the server can give. Space limitations in this book do not allow a comprehensive discussion of how to improve performance, profits and productivity in the kitchen.

Welcome to a perfect world ... and watch your step!

In a perfect world restaurant: Servers, busers, cooks and dishwashers never break a dish, a glass, or throw away silverware, ramekins, napkins or clean, unused butter, sugar, jelly or cracker packets.

In the perfect world bar the bartender uses a jigger to measure the liquor in every drink and pours every beer with a 3/4 inch foam head. Bartenders *never* run the tap before putting the beer glass under it ... in the perfect world. Cocktail servers cut just enough fruit so that it never spoils but is always fresh.

Over in the perfect world kitchen, the kitchen crew carefully checks every delivery item against the invoice for quality and correct price, obsessively stores and rotates perishables and dry goods with a first in-first out,

▼   ▼   ▼   ▼

last in-last out system and searches for opportunities to maximize the prep crew's performance and transform yesterday's special into today's soup du jour. Our cooks follow the exact recipes to the ounce and teaspoonful and use portion control and scales for every food and beverage item they prepare.

● ● ● ● ● ● ● ● ● ● ● ● ● ● ● ● ● ●
Wake up and go to sleep.
● ● ● ● ● ● ● ● ● ● ● ● ● ● ● ● ● ●

The perfect world manager greets every guest by name with a radiant smile that comes from knowing that labor costs are running at 9 percent, food costs at 21 percent, sales are up 81 percent over last year's and that their perfectly-trained staff will voluntarily clock out when there are too many people on the hourly payroll with too little to do. Oh, and no one *ever* calls in sick.

...brrring!

The sound you just heard is the clanging of the alarm clock that's waking you up from this "perfect world" dream. But it was fun while it lasted, wasn't it?

Now how 'bout a reality check?

Did you know you were making a fortune?

If you asked your servers, cooks, busers, host staff (or even certain managers) what they thought the average profit on the dollar is in the restaurant business, how do you think they'd reply? 70¢? 50¢? 35¢? 20¢? In our popular "Waste Watching" seminar we always ask this question of our audience. We're willing to bet you a dollar to a donut that the lowest answer you'll get from a server or hourly cook is that the restaurateur makes at least 25¢ on each dollar!

Fact: *The majority of restaurant employees believe that the restaurant owner is making a fortune.* They think that the menu price (or gross sales) goes directly into the operator's pocket, less maybe ten or fifteen percent, which goes to

• • • • • • • • • • • • • • • • • • •
Restaurateurs make less than a nickel on each dollar
• • • • • • • • • • • • • • • • • • •

cover costs. We wish. *You* wish. But "wishing" don't pay the bill collectors or the bank. How low *is* the national pre-tax full service restaurant average profit on the dollar nationwide?

4.7¢!!!
(cited in a recent American Express Briefing Newsletter)

Less than a nickel!! And remember, this is an *average*; some full-service restaurants are making maybe twelve cents (pre-tax) on the dollar, others are making .01 cents (pre-tax) on each buck they take in (that's one penny profit for every hundred dollars in sales!). Incidentally, the lower end numbers reflect the typical earnings for many of the full-service restaurant chains.

For those of you who were thinking of opening your own restaurant someday, the 4.7¢ figure should make you blanch, and possibly reconsider the business opportunities available at your local racetrack. Let's look at some of the typical fixed costs that a full-service restaurant is responsible for *daily*, whether a thousand people walk through the front door or no one does:

❖ all the food,

❖ all the beverage,

❖ labor (cooks, servers, managers, bookkeepers, busers, cleaning crew),

▼   ▼   ▼   ▼

❖   building maintenance,

❖   utilities (gas, heat, water, electricity),

❖   lease interest or mortgage payments,

❖   insurance (general liability, liquor liability),

❖   dry goods (silverware, flatware, glasses, nap-kins, detergent, etcetera),

❖   repairs and maintenance,

❖   Taxes!

Remember, these are daily fixed costs. When customers order entrees in your restaurant they are barely covering the cost of the owner **buying, storing, preparing, garnishing and serving** that food or beverage. *Suggesting and selling appetizers, sides, wines, desserts and drinks is often the dividing line between whether a restaurant even makes a profit or not.* Controlling costs and watching waste are the keys to assuring that profit. Making sales is the nail. Controlling costs is the hammer.

> *"Making big bucks in the service business isn't that hard. First, learn how to make money faster than you can spend it. From there on, it's easy"*
>
> — George Mannion

The employee, not the owner, runs the business

In addition to making sales, the successful restaurateur must simultaneously become an insatiable waste-watcher and — even more importantly — **teach his or her staff to be similarly obsessed.** What your staff doesn't know will hurt you. If you have daily pre-shift team meetings, be sure that waste-watching and food costs are daily topics along with service and sales skills. To insure your 4.7¢ average cut on each dollar you must not only train your staff to be salespeople but also teach them:

1. How to safely handle your physical inventory to minimize breakage (of glasses, plates, dishes, mixers, fryers, etetera).

2. How to *not* block drains in the kitchen (sky-high plumbing bills are a chronic illness in the restaurant business).

3. Why we must *not* routinely throw away unopened or unused:
   - sugar packets,
   - artificial sweetener packets,
   - creamers,
   - crackers,
   - butter,
   - jellies,
   - ketchup, mustard, dressings, etcetera

4. And while you're at it, point out that it's also not a good idea to throw away:
   - knives
   - forks
   - spoons
   - ramekins
   - cocktail forks
   - napkins
   - dishes, bowls or glasses

If you're an owner, operator or manager, wouldn't you just love to come to work one day and not have a server ask, *"Can we open some more silverware?"*

▼   ▼   ▼   ▼

The forty burger plate

Here's a little math that might drive home the importance of cost control relative to making sales. Let's round up the 4.7¢ national average profit and assume the restaurateur nets 5¢ on every dollar. Their restaurant offers a half-pound cheeseburger with fries for $5.00. That means the owner nets 25¢ for each hamburger platter sold (pre-tax). With us so far? Good.

Now let's assume that a server drops and breaks a plate that wholesales for $10. *How many burger platters do you now have to sell to pay for that $10 broken plate?*

40!

That's right, *forty* burgers!

How many $5 burgers do you have to sell if a bartender breaks a 14-ounce water/iced-tea/beer glass that wholesales for $1? Four burgers! *Just to pay for the glass!*

Q: So if you sell forty burgers at lunch and break one $10 plate or ten $1 glasses what else have you broken?

A: *Even!* The more careless your staff is with your tableware and glasses means the better you'll have to train them to sell *and sell lots!*

If you don't take the time to train your staff to be waste watchers, they're not gonna figure it out on their own. They think you're making a fortune. Who cares if another glass breaks? Have you ever been in a restaurant where someone on the staff *doesn't* laugh or applaud when a glass meets the floor with a resounding crash?

You walk by your raise or bonus every morning.

Every morning 99 percent of your staff routinely walks past that eight-box-high stack of produce, meats, cheese, etcetera, that's been delivered to the kitchen and they never give a thought to who pays for it. They may assume that the United Way drops it off and tells the manager, "No charge! Thanks to you it works for all of us!" Who *does* pay for it? Hopefully, the guest. But remember, customers don't *buy* things, they are *sold* things.

It takes daily coaching, teaching and training to get everyone on your staff to be "waste watchers." **What you reinforce is what you get. What you don't reinforce is what you lose!**

Here's an action plan you can use to start training your staff immediately in the principles of cost control and waste-watching:

How to train your employees to be waste watchers

Train your service staff

1. Set up regularly scheduled cost control seminars for your service staff. Teach them how to properly load and unload bustubs, stack dishes, scrape plates so you don't lose flatware or napkins in the trash, etcetera. Include this information in all your training manuals. Test the transfer of knowledge through oral and written quizzes.

Train your kitchen crew

2. Present regular seminars to your kitchen staff on the importance of portion control, equipment maintenance, safety and proper storage, rotation and prep procedures that minimize waste and control costs. Include these ideas in their written training materials in both English and Spanish. Quiz and test them. Require all kitchen employees to score 90 percent or better.

Train your dishwasher

3. Nail an empty five-quart bucket to the wall by the dishwasher so he or she can throw dry, uncontaminated and unopened sugar, salt, pepper or

▼   ▼   ▼   ▼

How your dishwasher can save you $10,000 a year.

cracker packets into it that have been left on clean plates or bowls, mistakenly dropped off at the dishwashing area. Then reconcile the bucket's individual contents back to their proper storage places as the last thing the dishwasher does before leaving. Consider giving the dishwasher a cash bonus for each bucket he or she collects and reconciles. Again: What you reinforce is what you get.

Audit your garbage

4. Schedule a different employee to help a manager sift through a randomly selected garbage can at least once a week (every week) for items that shouldn't have been thrown away. Dig out the carelessly tossed cocktail forks, ramekins, knives, spoons and unopened sugar or cracker packets that should not have been thrown away in the first place. (Note: *Don't* re-use them!) Count up the cost of the broken physical inventory (glasses, plates, bowls) or re-usable items that have been thrown away in the one trash can. Then multiply that figure times all the trash cans you emptied that night. Now ... pour yourself a stiff drink! You'll find out not only what your employees like to throw away, but you'll also learn what your guests don't like to eat (maybe cream of spinach is a bad choice as vegetable of the month!) We first heard this idea from trainer Jim Moffa who also said: "You can learn a lot by hanging around the dirty end of a dish machine!"

"If I were setting up an apartment, I'd sure know where to look!"

Catch the waste before it gets to the dump

5. Buy the commercially available magnetic "traps" that fit over your kitchen's garbage cans to help catch "accidentally" tossed flatware. Or use clear trash bags.

Consider using a special waste bucket

6. Choose a specific color waste bucket and use it in the kitchen for food that was prepared or ordered incorrectly and had to be thrown away. Review the contents after each shift with the kitchen crew and tally up the dollar amount wasted. Set specific cash bonuses for a zero-mistakes shift goal. (Careful with this one. Savvy cooks or servers soon learn to "bury their mistakes" in the recesses of the "generic" trash cans. It's worth a try, though.)

Publicize the costs

7. Mount samples of your glasses, dishes, flatware, napkins, etcetera, on a piece of plywood with their price posted next to each item. Put this in a conspicuous high-traffic location in your kitchen. Point out to your employees that this is their raise they're throwing away when they're careless.

Team bonus

8. Consider giving a team bonus to your service and kitchen crew for lowering breakage or food costs. First determine how much your monthly physical inventory is costing you. Challenge the crew to lower that by 50 percent. Offer 20 percent of the money saved as a cash bonus to the staff to be shared as a team.

Recycle your glass products

9. Many companies will pay you a penny a bottle for your recyclable glass. Look in your Yellow Pages under "recycling."

▼   ▼   ▼   ▼

Watch water waste

10. Train your prep people and kitchen crew to try to anticipate frozen items that need to be thawed and thaw them in the refrigerator, not under six hours of running tap water!

Money down the toilet

11. Fill an empty two-quart sour cream container with water and place it in the back of your toilet tank. You'll use less water to flush.

No more free pour

12. Provide and require the use of a jigger for every cocktail your bartender makes. Does your gas station let you "free pour" ten dollars worth of gas?

• • • • • • • • • • • • • • • • • • •

"The foodservice industry is the only business I know where there's more ways to lose money than make money."

— *Matt Jones*

• • • • • • • • • • • • • • • • • • •

Don't "eyeball" your specs

13. Don't let your cooks or prep people "eyeball" the correct portions of your food recipes (same as the gas station example above). Have plenty of scales handy to expedite this practice. More importantly, check obsessively to make sure they're *using* those scales. **Remember: you get what you inspect, not what you expect.**

Reward waste watching

14. Offer a monthly plaque, trophy, gift certificate or cash award to the best cost-saving employee idea.

The key here is to reinforce a different method of "waste-watching" every day at your pre-shift team meetings for both service staff and kitchen crew. Set *specific* waste-watching or cost-control goals each shift. What you reinforce is what you get. What you don't reinforce is what you lose!

▼　　▼　　▼

How many of you have ever been bitten by an *elephant?* Well then, how many of you have ever been bitten by a *mosquito?* Hmm. Suspicions confirmed; *it's not the "big" things that eat us alive in this business, it's the little things.*

COURSE 5: After Dinner Drinks
"Something to wash it all down"

No train? No gain.

It never ceases to amaze us how many different and sometimes bizarre methods restaurateurs will use to boost sagging customer counts and slow business. They'll invest huge sums of money trying to advertise and promote their restaurant or bar in a wild variety of schemes ranging from the ridiculous to the sublime, from full page newspaper ads to a

• •

> *"If you think training is*
> *expensive, try ignorance."*
> — *NEA slogan*

• •

balloon-toting clown on the street waving traffic into their parking lot.

If you want to improve your business, hold off on renting the Goodyear blimp for now and *invest your advertising and promotion dollars into training instead.* Before you say "yeah, but .... " think for a second about how important training, teaching and coaching is in your everyday life.

   ◆ How'd you learn to tie your shoes?
   ◆ To ride a bike? Ski? Play the piano?
   ◆ Open a bottle of wine?
   ◆ Mix a margarita?

Somebody showed you how, then you practiced. And screwed it up. Then practiced some more. Someone showed you again. You practiced more, screwed it up less, and finally, you *got* it. Would you bet on a football team that doesn't practice? You wouldn't. If you have children, how did you choose the neighbor-

▼　　▼　　▼　　▼

hood you live in? Probably based on the quality of the schools your kids will attend. We put such a premium on education in our non-working world, so why do we think that educating our employees is any less beneficial for them and our business?

Look, we know that time is one of our most precious resources and that it's the one thing we seem to have so little of in this business. *But we must find and take the time to train and train well.* Like Grandpa Sullivan used to say: "If you ain't got time to do it right, when will you have time to do it over?"

. . . .
Do you want to do it right or do it over?
. . . .

Fact: Training is a *daily* obligation of restaurant managers. **It is your duty as supervisors to teach everyone on your staff something new every day.** The only thing an owner *really* has in a restaurant is the skill level of his or her employees.

Tie one on....

We've got to be honest with you for a second. It's been our experience that asking most managers to add teaching and training to their already long list of duties is like asking a guy in an electric chair if he'd prefer AC or DC.

One reason many restaurateurs shy away from daily training (especially with their "pros" or "seasoned" veterans) is because it seems to take so long to *see results.* Which reminds us of a story....

A helicopter pilot crashes in the Sahara desert with no food or water. He crawls for two days across the blazing sand. There's no apparent hope in sight. Suddenly he sees a Sheik carrying a suitcase a dune away walking toward him. The pilot staggers up to the man and begs for a drink of water. "Sorry, I have no water," says the Sheik, "but I *do* have a great selection of Italian silk ties in this suitcase. Only $3 each, or two for $5. Would you like one?"

The pilot was dumbfounded. "No! I need water, water! Where can I find some?"

The Sheik gestured eastward and said, "There's a restaurant two dunes over that sells plenty of water ... you sure you don't want to buy a tie?"

The pilot pushed the Sheik aside. "Are you crazy? Get out of my way!" And he stumbled off in the direction of the bistro. Soon he saw the restaurant. It had a large outdoor patio that was packed with people drinking Perrier, beer, martinis, frozen margaritas and wine. He dusted himself off and reached for the door knob. Suddenly a large bouncer in a tuxedo tapped him on the shoulder.

"Can I help you sir?" the bouncer asked.

"Yes!" blubbered the exasperated pilot. "I want some water!"

"Sorry, sir," the bouncer said, gingerly picking the pilot up by the collar and turning him around, *"no admittance without a tie!"*

Moral: *The most difficult decision you'll make today is the one that won't affect you until tomorrow.*

Why train every day? It may take one day or six months to see any results in your staff. Why? Because eventually you *will* see results. The restaurateur who doesn't train, *doesn't try* and never *will* see any results. *Nothing ventured, nothing gained.*

Think of training as farming or gardening. First you prepare the soil (orientation). Then you plant the seeds (training manuals and videos). Then you fertilize (daily coaching). Then you water (daily training). And then you wait. And wait and wait and *wait. Finally* the crop comes up for you (higher sales and better service). You eat, you thrive. But not without commitment and cultivation. Every seed must have a gardener. Every manager is a farmer.

> *It's not what's poured into an employee, it's what's planted that counts!*

▼　　▼　　▼　　▼

Forget your employees' "attitudes." Work instead on their behavior.

All of the skills associated with great service and suggestive selling are *behavioral* in nature. If your training manuals demand that your employees have a "positive attitude," good luck, because **you can't change anyone's attitude without first changing their behavior!**

The goal of training should always be to change behavior. Think about it.

Would you rather have your servers demonstrat-

• • • • • • • • • • • • • • • • •

A farmer not a manager.

• • • • • • • • • • • • • • • • •

ing *behavior* like pulling out guests' chairs, hanging up their coats, learning and using your guests' names, suggesting appetizers, sides and desserts and smiling and thanking your guests. Or would you rather have them walking around with a "good attitude" but venturing no farther out on the Branch of Hospitality than "Are you ready to order?" Which employee is going to please your guest more?

This, in our opinion, is why 99 percent of all restaurant training fails. We call it "Teflon Training": training that won't stick. Most operators focus on trying to change their employees' attitudes instead of their behavior. This never works, because **people can repeat their behavior, but no one can repeat their attitude.** Author Ken Blanchard offered the best example we've heard: "my *attitude* is that I'm on a diet. My *behavior* this morning was to eat three chocolate donuts. Now what's going to make me lose weight? Changing my *attitude* or changing my *behavior?*"

What will improve your service and increase your sales? Changing your waitstaff's attitude or their behavior? Remember diet versus donuts!

"The greatest enemy of training outside the classroom is habit," says seminar leader Bob Pike. And right he is.

They say it takes twenty-one days of different behavior to change a habit. If you want to change bad habits and bad attitudes work on the behavior first.

Put this book down and fold your arms across your chest. Look down at which arm is on top. Now, reverse the position of those arms, folding them again. Feels funny, doesn't it? Now, fold your hands. Note which thumb is on top. Reverse the order. Doesn't that feel strange, abnormal? Well, everybody folds their arms or hands a certain way and everybody feels that *their* way of doing it is the *right* way. But there is no "right" way, we're merely folding arms and fingers. Yet how hard would it be for you to change the way you presently fold your arms or fingers? This is an example of how attitude ("this is the right way") reinforces behavior ("folding fingers"), whether right or wrong. This is important to know. Why?

Next time you try to change someone else's habits remember how hard it is to change your own!

You can't change an order-taker's habits overnight, but you won't change them at all unless you start trying.

● ●
Eliminating "teflon" training.
● ●

The ten commitments of effective foodservice incentives

In the last five years Pencom has presented 600 live service and sales training seminars to 100,000 foodservice employees in 48 states and seven countries. If there's one area that our audiences continually face challenges with, and want to know more about, it's how to implement effective contests, incentives and rewards for their employees and managers. And now that you've read hundreds of ways to improve your service, sales, food costs, teamwork and marketing skills, let's talk about ways to create realistic and cost-effective incentives to help ensure that your employees will be *self-motivated to deliver* better service, produce higher sales and lower your operating costs.

We implemented employee incentives ten years ago in our five Denver restaurants and bars. Through expert advice from companies like Wal-Mart, Walt Disney and our own trial and error, we've designed successful programs for our servers, kitchen crew, host staff and managers. Once we fine-tuned the programs and then tracked the positive results for five years, we helped implement over thirty other incentives, contests and reward systems for sixty different foodservice and retail clients nationwide. Incentives can be your greatest asset ... and a significant liability if you don't use them properly.

> *"Is it ignorance or apathy that causes restaurant managers to ignore training? Well, I don't know and I don't care."*
> — Michael Feeney

Most of my fellow operators, trainers and managers feel like the proverbial mosquito in a nudist camp when it comes to employee incentives; they know exactly what they want to do, but where do they start? Here's how.

We'd like to suggest the following basic guidelines relative to implementing effective foodservice incentives, contests and rewards in *your* operation:

1. **Understand that you cannot "motivate" anyone.**
   You can, however, **create an environment in which your employees are self-motivated**. To do what? Improve performance, profits and productivity. Effective incentives are a key factor to help create a self-motivated waitstaff and kitchen crew.

2. Remember that people will do more to avoid pain than to gain pleasure.

This means that your contest or incentive goal must be perceived as being reasonably attainable and should encourage your employees to work smarter, not necessarily harder. If, for instance, a sales contest goal is to raise guest checks an average of $2 per person, many servers may feel they have to be too pushy and therefore risk the perceived "pain" of more resistance and rejection from their customers. The higher tips or color TV prize a month away may not offset the daily frustration. Instead, set your sights lower to one dollar per person. Point out that this equals selling only one beverage to one guest or four people splitting a $3.95 appetizer. The goal is less painful, more pleasurable. *Gradually* raise the hurdle. Crawl, walk, run. *Break your sales or service goals into the lowest common denominators.* If, for instance, you want to increase appetizer sales by 10 percent this month, present the goal to your staff in terms of 1200 more appetizers per month, or 40 per day, 20 per shift, or only two per server, per section. Sounds a lot more do-able than "1200 appetizers" or "10 percent," doesn't it? Inspire the staff to see the goal in terms of how they can help achieve it daily.

3. Keep it short and simple.

Our experience has shown that contests for hourly workers get the best results when they are held, measured and rewarded within a 30-day period. People tend to lose interest after a month. If you want to use the same contest format again because you're pleased with the results, reintroduce it the very next month with new rewards after 30 days.

▼   ▼   ▼   ▼

4. **With incentives, as with medicine, prescription before diagnosis is malpractice.**
Don't put the cart before the horse. Make certain that the behavior pattern you're trying to change can be resolved with an incentive program or contest. It could be that your performance (or lack of performance) challenge is actually a *training* problem. Before people can **exceed** performance they have to first be thoroughly **trained** to perform. The result of poor training is confusion; confused people will not act.

5. **Don't just stare up the steps, you must step up the stairs.**
Determine your goals, create incentives to help achieve them, evaluate your progress weekly and encourage your staff daily. The vision must be followed by venture. You can't steal second or third base from the batter's box, or with a foot planted on first. Check the progress with every staff member weekly. You get what you inspect, not what you expect. As restaurateur Mike Amos says, "What gets measured, gets done."

6. **Manage results, not just activities.**
Structure your incentive programs for a 10:1 return-on-investment ratio. For every dollar you spend on an incentive program or sales contest, expect a minimum return of ten dollars in money saved (such as a safety contest) or sales generated (such as a highest check average contest). Every contest should have a "carrot" and a "stick." Reward the people who achieve the incentive goals and retrain the ones who don't. Offer them extra coaching and counseling. The "stick" is for moving them along the right path, not for beating their backsides.

7. Incentive programs are a team effort.

Think of ways to involve every department when setting up sales, service or safety contests or incentives. Using the appetizer incentive and goal (in step #2 on page 103,) be certain that you identify everyone involved in the process of merchandising appetizers to your guests. This list would include host staff, servers, bartenders, cooks, prep cooks and managers. We'll assume that the contest format you've chosen will result in an increase in appetizer sales. So what's in it for the prep cooks to make more appetizers? What's in it for the cooks to get the appetizers out quickly? What's in it for the host staff to consistently suggest appetizers to every guest they seat? Granted, one could answer that "they get to keep their jobs!" But if you're creating incentives and prizes for the waitstaff to sell more, remember that your kitchen staff may be thinking, "why should I bust my butt when *they* win all the prizes?" Prep cooks can be rewarded for zero mistakes, kitchen crew for consistently getting the apps out under five minutes and servers for the number of appetizers sold.

8. The way to get employees past a problem is to get them involved in the solution.

None of us is as smart as all of us. If you have a problem with poor service, high costs or low sales, gather your staff together. Present the challenges to them, break them into teams and ask smart questions like, *"What can we change to improve our service, lower our cost and increase our sales?"* or *"What are some of the reasons we're experiencing these problems now?"* People don't argue with their own data. Encourage them to brainstorm as many solutions as possible in 15 minutes. Award the team generating the most ideas with individual one dollar lotto "quick-picks" for their "million-dollar" contributions.

9. Award merchandise, not cash, to prize winners.
Merchandise can't be spent and it has a "trophy" value. It is cost-effective; you can trade out restaurant gift certificates for goods or services from local merchants. They need prizes for contests, too. Ask your staff what kinds of prizes they'd work for. Don't forget to think about what their families would like to use when you're choosing appropriate merchandise for rewards.

10. Structure sales contests to generate several winners.
For waitstaff, reward not only the highest check average or highest sales per hour, but also the most-improved sales percentage. This helps eliminate the "same-server-always-wins" syndrome. Post and update your check averages and sales results weekly, including each server's "personal best" high check average. Reward the servers who exceed their personal best every week. For kitchen contests, reward each member based on total hours worked within the contest or incentive's time frame.

There are many considerations affecting a cost-effective and revenue-generating incentive program, and these are ten points to consider. But how about an example of a contest you can use immediately to demonstrate how well they work? Here's one you can implement the minute you're done reading this: We call it the *"Floating Twenty Dollar Bill."* Here's how it works:

Choose a menu or beverage item you want to sell during a normally busy shift, like nachos, bowls of soup, cheesecake with strawberries or glasses of premium wine. The first server to sell **one** is presented with a $20 bill. The first server to sell **two** takes the $20 from the server who sold one. The seller of **three** appropriates the $20 from the server who sold two. This exchange continues through the entire shift from server to server for a pre-set time determined by the manager. The end result? *Everyone* increases their sales and has fun doing so for a minimal investment ($20) by management. This contest also works well at lunch with a ten-dollar incentive.

Well, there you have it. Obviously we were "self-motivated" enough to save, share and write these ideas down for your perusal. We hope we've created an incentive for you to *use* them. Well done is better than well said.

● ●

During the Depression a 10-year old boy entered a hotel coffee shop and asked a waitress: "How much is an ice cream sundae?"

"Fifty cents," she replied.

The little boy looked over the change in his hand. "How much is a dish of plain ice cream?" he asked.

Other customers were now waiting for a table and the waitress was a bit impatient. "Thirty-five cents," she snapped.

The little boy again counted the coins. "I'll have the plain ice cream," he said.

The waitress brought the ice cream, put the bill on the table, and walked away. The boy fin-ished the ice cream, paid the cashier, and departed.

When the waitress returned, she picked up the empty plate and then swallowed hard at what she saw. There, placed neatly beside the empty dish, were two nickels and five pennies — her tip.

— *Contributed by Dan Rather*

COURSE 6: Check Please
"Putting it all together"

A tale of two restaurants
Chapter One

It's 3:15 p.m. on a Friday afternoon in Anytown, U.S.A.

Jerry M. has just finished talking on the phone to his wife, Joan, from his office at the Acme Widget Company. Yes, the baby-sitter can be at their house by 6:30. Yes, Jerry will call and confirm their dinner reservations for 7:30 at the Hillside Inn and no, Joan won't have any trouble being ready by 7 p.m.

Jerry's been excited about this night all week. Rarely do he and his wife get out together since the baby came. Besides, this will give Jerry a chance to check out the Hillside Inn he's heard so much about.

• •

Real marketing begins when the guest walks in.

• •

Jerry's a candidate for the new District Manager position at the Acme Widget company. The vice president of sales, the "Big Boss," Mr. Larkin, will be in town next Thursday to personally interview Jerry for the position. He's asked Jerry to pick a restaurant where they can have a good dinner and talk over business. Having never been out with the "big boss" before, Jerry decided to visit the Hillside Inn with Joan first. He doesn't want to blow the chance for a promotion by picking the wrong environment.

Jerry's colleague Sam has been offered the same position and Mr. Larkin has asked him to also choose a restaurant for dinner. Sam will be taking his boss out Monday night. Jerry gets his opportunity Tues-

▼   ▼   ▼   ▼

day evening. Since Jerry's and Sam's track records are nearly identical, Jerry knows that the way he handles himself at dinner could decide if he — or Sam — gets the promotion.

Better call to confirm that 7:30 reservation.

"Hello!" the cheery voice on the other end of the phone answers after two rings.

Jerry pauses. Did he get the wrong number? *"Hi ... is this 837-0334 ... the Hillside restaurant?"*

"Oh! Sorry! Yeah it is," the voice giggles. *"Kineyeelp you?"*

"Yeah, this is Jerry Mathers. I wanted to confirm a reservation for two at 7:30 tonight, please...."

"Jussasecond," the voice replies, and Jerry's on hold.

So Jerry waits. And waits. And waits. He begins to drum his fingers on his desktop. Finally, the phone clicks again.

"Hillside Inn, may I help you?" It's a new voice.

"Yes," Jerry says, doing his best to sound calm. *"I'm trying to confirm a reservation for two, for Mathers, at 7:30 tonight."*

"Jussasecond." Click. Hold. Another click. Suddenly, a dial tone. He's been disconnected.

Jerry opens the phone book again, looks up the Hillside number and dials. The phone rings six times. Someone finally picks it up. *"Hillside Inn kin you hold?"* Click.

Thirty seconds go by. A minute passes. Jerry's face is turning redder than a turkey's rump at pokeberry time. After what seems to be an eternity, another click and a cheery voice asks: *"Hillside Inn, this is Jill, can I help you?"* Jerry grits his teeth and repeats his request one more time. *"Oh yes sir, we have it right here,"* the voice assures him. *"Mr. Mathers. 7:30. Right?"*

"Right, good. Um ... a quick question," Jerry asks. *"How do you get there from downtown?"*

"I'm not sure. Let me put you on hold for just a---"

But Jerry knows better and hangs up first.

Chapter Two

Excited about going out, Jerry and Joan dress up for the occasion and give the baby-sitter last minute instructions along with the Hillside's phone number.

They call a neighbor, get directions to the restaurant and pull into the Hillside's crowded parking lot at 7:20. As they approach the entrance they notice two empty beer bottles in the parking lot. Joan picks them up and puts them on the curb. *"Don't wanna run over them on the way out."*

A soda can is lying in the planter by the door. As Jerry reaches for the handle, three departing guests suddenly push open the front door from the inside and the Mathers quickly step back to avoid being hit.

Stepping into the Hillside's foyer, they notice several empty mint and toothpick wrappers lying on the floor next to the leaves that have blown in. They open the second set of doors and enter the busy restaurant.

Chapter Three

The joint is jumping. In the midst of all the action, anxiously waiting guests are huddled in groups of two and three by the front door and hostess stand. Waiters and waitresses scurry by, arms laden with food and drink-filled trays. The hostess is standing behind a huge lectern-like stand, two steps up from the main floor, her head buried in and her hand scribbling on the reservation book. A large sign cau-

▼   ▼   ▼   ▼

tions the Mathers to *"Please wait to be seated."*

Jerry tries to establish some eye contact with the hostess. After all, the sign didn't say *"Please wait to be acknowledged!"* Having little success getting her attention, he walks up to her and says, *"Excuse me...."* Just then the phone rings. The hostess raises her index finger at Jerry, and quickly answers the phone. It rings again. And again. She adroitly puts three people on hold and turns to Jerry with an expressionless *"Can I help you sir?"*

"Mathers. Two. Seven-thirty reservations?" he says.

The hostess looks at her reservation list, then left, then right. *"We're running a little behind, sir. There's a 20-minute wait. Have a seat at the bar and we'll get you when your table is ready, okay?"*

"But I had a reserv---" Jerry's protest is cut off as the hostess dashes away, presumably in search of a waiting party whose table is ready. He works his way through the staring, waiting crowd back to his wife.

"They won't have our table for 15 or 20 more minutes," Jerry glumly tells Joan.

"That's okay, honey," she replies, *"it's busy for a reason ... must be good. Let's get a drink."*

"Awright," Jerry agrees, and they make their way to the crowded bar.

Chapter Four

They luck out and grab two bar stools that have just been vacated. The bartender closest to them has his head and eyes in the bar sinks, busily washing stacks of beer, wine and "rocks" glasses. Jerry waits. A minute goes by. The bartender continues washing. Finally Jerry yells, *"Excuse me! Can we get a drink?"*

The bartender looks up, wipes his hands on his apron and sidles over to the couple. He smiles and asks, *"What kin I getcha?"*

"A glass of chardonnay, please," Joan says. The smiling bartender nods and then looks at her husband.

"What kind of beers do you have?" Jerry asks.

The bartender jerks his thumb upward to a row of different-labeled beer bottles balanced on a top shelf of the bar. *"They're up there,"* he replies.

Since he can't make out the labels on the beer bottles, Jerry decides to order a rum and coke.

"Rum 'n coke and a chardonnay," the bartender says and starts to move away.

"Oh ... wait!" Jerry yells after the bartender. *"Do you have Bacardi Black rum?"*

"Yeah," the bartender replies. *"I think so."*

"I'll have that instead of the well rum," says Jerry. The bartender pauses. *"That's extra,"* he says.

"So?" says Jerry. His wife pats him on the hand. He relaxes a little.

On his way to make the drinks, the bartender sees a customer that he hadn't recognized before. The bartender smiles broadly, his face beaming like the seat of a bus driver's pants. *"Joe!"* he yells, his hand extended to the patron, *"long time no see, buddy!"* The bartender suddenly launches into an animated conversation about jet skiing. Two minutes later he mixes and delivers the Mathers' drinks.

"Here you go. Six-fifty please," he says as he sets the drinks down in front of Jerry and Joan.

"Can you start me a tab, please?" Jerry asks.

The bartender pauses. *"Ummm ... well ... yeah, I could. But if you don't mind, I'll be getting off in a few minutes.... Can you just pay for this round now, and then I'll have the other bartender start you a tab on your next drinks?"*

▼   ▼   ▼   ▼

Jerry and Joan exchange looks. *"Yeah,"* Jerry sighs. *"Alright."* He throws down a ten.

The bartender rings up the drinks, slaps Jerry's change back on the bar and says, *"Thanks, guy."* Jerry reluctantly pushes a dollar tip back.

"Let's look at the appetizers," Joan says brightly. She asks the bartender if he has an appetizer list. He looks up from his conversation with Joe. *"Uh ... yeah ... somewhere. Let me see if I can get one from the hostess. It might be a minute...."*

Joan and Jerry exchange a look.

"Oh, that's okay. Never mind," she tells the bartender. *"Let's wait till we get our table,"* she says to Jerry. He shrugs.

Chapter Five

"Mr. Mathers? Your table is ready," A smiling hostess suddenly appears behind Jerry and Joan.

"Oh! Great. Good," says Jerry. The hostess watches them as they grab their coats and drinks and cheerfully says, *"This way please."*

The hostess glides through the crowded dining room and arrives at the freshly-bused table ahead of her guests. When the Mathers get to the table, the hostess drops the menus, smiles and watches Jerry pull out Joan's chair and hang up her coat.

Once they're seated, the hostess hands the couple their menus and cheerfully says, *"Our dinner specials are listed on the board over there and your waitress's name is Sharon. Enjoy!"*

"Thanks," says Jerry. He and his wife look around the busy dining room. It's already 8:05 but the wait seems to be worth it judging by the happy-looking customers around him.

"Can you read those specials from here?" asks Joan.

Jerry squints. *"Not really."* he says. *"We can ask our waitress."* He and his wife join hands, exchange a quick kiss and begin to peruse the menu.

▼   ▼   ▼   ▼

Chapter Six

Two minutes later, a buser appears at the table. He fills the Mathers' water glasses. *"Excuse me, where's the bathroom?"* Joan asks.

The buser points across the dining room, *"Over there by the staircase, ma'am."* He smiles and exits.

Joan gets up. *"I'll be right back. Order me another glass of chardonnay, honey."* Joan stops at the hostess stand to find out where that staircase is that the buser gestured at. *"Right over there by the phones,"* the hostess says in a tiny voice, pointing the way before picking up the microphone and booming over the P.A. system: *"Jones ... Party of six!!"* The sudden loudness causes Jerry to drop his menu and a dog across the street to drop his bone. Two minutes pass.

Chapter Seven

"Hi! I'm Sharon. Just one tonight?" The waitress's cheery voice takes Jerry by surprise.

"Uh ... no, no. My wife went to the ladies room."

"Can I get you something from the bar, to start?" He orders two glasses of chardonnay.

"House or premium?" the waitress asks. *"Our premium wines by the glass are listed there."* She points at a table tent next to the salt shaker.

Jerry glances at the table tent then back at his waitress. *"Um. Just house, I guess. That's fine."*

The waitress scribbles on her pad. *"Great. Be right back with those."* She walks over to the next table. *"Ready to order, gentlemen?"* she asks the four men in business suits.

Joan returns and picks up her menu. *"What looks good, honey?"* She takes a corner of her napkin and wipes off the dried gravy spot off her menu.

"I don't know," Jerry says. *"Maybe the swordfish. The fried chicken sounds good, too. How 'bout you?"*

Joan smiles. *"Don't know. It all looks good. Pasta Alfredo ... or a filet. I haven't had a steak in a while."*

The waitress returns with the two glasses of wine.

"Are you guys ready to order or do you need a few more minutes?"

"I guess I'll just have the small filet, medium rare," says Joan.

"I'll try the swordfish."

"The swordfish and the petite filet," the waitress says. *"Did you want an appetizer to start, or...."* her voice trails off. Jerry and Joan look at each other, then back at their menus. Sharon waits patiently.

"No ... I guess not," says Jerry.

Sharon turns to Joan. *"How 'bout you ma'am?"*

"Well ... no. No, I don't think so," says Joan. She quickly glances over the menu, closes it, and hands it over to Sharon.

"Okay. Thanks!" says Sharon. She leaves to turn their orders in.

"I thought you liked sauteed mushrooms on your steak?" Jerry asks.

"I didn't see them on the menu. Did they have 'em?" Joan asks.

"Yeah, under the appetizers," says Jerry.

Chapter Eight

Sharon brings out the dinner salads in about five minutes.

Fifteen minutes later, the entrees arrive. Jerry's swordfish is delicious. Joan loves her salad, but the filet is grilled more medium than medium-rare. She thinks that it is easier to eat it and not complain than it is to try to get the waitress's attention. Sharon is awfully busy with a party of twelve people next to them.

Sharon eventually gets a break from her large party and greets the Mathers. *"Sorry. I got really swamped there. How was everything?"* she asks, picking up the dirty plates.

"Well my steak was a little overdone," says Joan. *"But no big deal."*

"I'm not surprised," says Sharon, *"our kitchen has*

been messing up orders all night. I apologize. Would you like me to get a manager?"

"No. No need." says Joan.

"Okay. Sorry 'bout that!" Sharon said, picking up the rest of their dirty plates. *"Some dessert tonight or are you guys too full?"*

Jerry and Joan exchange glances. *"What do you think Mr. Sweet Tooth?"* Joan asks.

Jerry shakes his head. *"If I eat dessert I'll have to run an extra mile and a half tomorrow."*

"So?" his wife says. *"Me too."*

Sharon looks nervously over at her twelve-top. *"Tell you what, I'll give you a few minutes to decide."* She says and starts to leave.

"Um ... ma'am?" Jerry says. Sharon turns. *"You can just bring us the check, okay?"*

"Sure," Sharon replies. *"Save room for dessert next time! Two coffees?"*

"Yeah," says Jerry, *"thanks."*

Five minutes later Sharon delivers the coffees and the tab. *"Thanks a lot, folks. I'll take this whenever you're ready!"* she says.

Jerry looks at his watch. It's 10:15 p.m. *"Wow, we better get going,"* he says, looking over the bill and then flipping a credit card onto the tip tray, *"we told Patti we'd be back by 10:30."* Five minutes pass. *"Where'd our waitress go?"* *"Dunno,"* says Joan.

Chapter Nine

Jerry's watch says 10:22 p.m. Sharon has still not returned to reconcile the bill. *"This is ridiculous,"* Jerry finally says. *"Do you see our waitress? Or a manager?"* He grabs his credit card and the tab and stands up.

"Where are you going?" asks Joan.

"To pay the darn tab!" he says, heading in the direction of the kitchen. Jerry finds Sharon in the wait station, smoking a cigarette and rolling silverware and napkin set ups.

"Scuse me," Jerry says, *"mind if we pay for this??"*
Embarrassed, Sharon leaps to her feet and stubs out her cigarette. *"I'm sorry, sir. I'll take care of that right away and bring it right back to you. Sorry."*

Jerry stomps back to his table, crosses his arms, knits his brow, plops into his chair ... and waits. *"Did you find her?"* Joan asks.

"Yeah," says Jerry. *"She was takin' a break."* He looks at his watch. *"It's 10:30! Cripes. We better call the baby-sitter and let her know we're on our way."*

"I'll do it," says Joan. *"Hang on, here she comes"* Jerry says. Sharon hustles up to the table with Jerry's check voucher.

"I'm very sorry, sir. Thank you. I didn't charge you for the coffees."

Jerry looks over the charges, writes in two dollars less on the tip, scribbles his signature and grumbles, *"Let's go."*

Chapter Ten

The restaurant is now slowly emptying. Busers are busing, servers are lounging, the manager is eating and the bartenders are counting their tips. Jerry pauses by the hostess stand to help Joan on with her coat. The hostess looks up from her phone conversation and smiles. Jerry smiles back halfheartedly and holds the door open for his wife. On the ride home, Jerry doesn't say much.

"C'mon!" says Joan. *"It wasn't that bad. The food was good. We finally got out together. Cheer up."*

"Yeah." Jerry mumbles. *"Okay. I guess you're right."*

Chapter Eleven

It's Monday morning at the Acme Widget Company.

Actually, it *wasn't* so bad last Friday night at the Hillside, Jerry thinks to himself. Except for the problem reconciling the check, the service was alright, or as good as it gets in most places. The food *was* pretty good. When he takes Mr. Larkin there tomorrow night, he'll just make sure that he hands the waitress his credit card as soon as she drops the check! Jerry wonders where Sam will be taking his boss for dinner tonight. He hopes he'll still have a shot at the job when it's his turn to impress the boss. He calls the Hillside to make reservations for 7 p.m. tomorrow night. The person who answers gets the reservations right the first time. Jerry feels better.

Chapter Twelve

Tuesday afternoon at the Acme Widget Company.

The entire sales staff has just been through a 90 minute sales meeting on the importance of customer service with the four district managers and Mr. Larkin. Sam seems awfully chummy with the big boss today, Jerry thinks to himself.

After the meeting Mr. Larkin walks up to Jerry *"Got a minute?"* he asks. *"I wanted to make sure we're still on for dinner."*

Oh, yeah, like I forgot. *"Of course. Mr. Larkin,"* Jerry says. *"Seven o'clock reservations okay?"*

"Perfect. Why don't you pick me up at the hotel around six-thirty. We can talk a little before dinner."

"Yes sir," says Jerry. Out of the corner of his eye he notices Sam walking up to them. *"By the way, how was your dinner last night, sir?"*

Mr. Larkin sat down on the corner of a table. *"Well,"* he began, *"if you really want to know, I think that restaurant should have sat in on our service seminar today."*

"How's that?" Jerry asked.

Mr. Larkin started ticking off the points on his fingers. *"We couldn't confirm our reservation in less than three phone calls. When we got there we had to wait a half-*

hour longer than our reservation time. The hostess wrote down our names but never used them. Our bartender couldn't take the time to tell us what kind of beers they had or recommend some appetizers but he had all the time in the world to tell a joke to his buddy while he ignored us. Do you want me to continue?" Mr. Larkin asked.

"It got worse?" Jerry asked, tickled at Sam's faux pas.

"Worse? If that restaurant was a fish I'd throw it back! The waiter never suggested wine or soup or garlic bread or even the onion rings that everybody else was eating. I also would've appreciated being presented some dessert options instead of 'you don't want any dessert, do you?' No liqueurs or after dinner drinks were mentioned or offered. I had to ask for a Grand Marnier. He didn't know what it was! On the way out I held the door open for us. I should've used them as a bad service example in our meeting today."

"Did you talk to a manager?" Jerry asked.

*"**Talk** to one?"* Mr. Larkin was exasperated. *"We never even **saw** one!"*

Just then Sam joined them. *"Hey, Jerry. Mr. Larkin. Great speech today, sir."*

"Thanks, Sam. I was just telling Larry here about our dinner last night," said Mr. Larkin.

"Where did you go?" Jerry asked Sam.

"Same place we've been going for years! The Hillside," Sam beamed. *"The food is good, but you really can't beat their service!"*

Mr. Larkin just stared at Sam for a long moment, then turned to Jerry. *"And where would you like to go for dinner tonight, Mathers?"*

"Well, sir, I understand the Valley View Grill is a great restaurant," he replied. *"That's where I made reservations."*

"Good. See you at 6:30." Mr. Larkin walked away.

Sam stared wide-eyed at Jerry. *"The Valley View Grill. Are you kidding me? This guy grades on service. The Valley View's isn't even close to the Hillside's! I guess the next time I see you, you'll be reporting to me!"*

Epilogue

The Valley View's service exceeded the Hillside's in every way. The hostess greeted Jerry and Mr. Larkin by name from the reservation list and recommended the nachos or Oysters Rockefeller as she sat them. The waiter described a medium-priced bottle of Pinot Noir that not only was on special that night, but complemented their steak entrees perfectly. The sauteed onions and mushrooms he suggested for the New York strips were mighty tasty. He encouraged them to save room for either the Mud Pie or praline ice cream, which they did.

The manager stopped by their table, introduced herself, asked their names, where they worked and offered each her business card, inviting them to call ahead anytime and she'd be sure they got special attention since Acme Widget employees were regular customers. She asked for their cards and made a note on the back to send them each a thank you note the next day. *"How about a Grand Marnier, Courvoisier or an Irish Coffee, gentlemen?"* the server had asked after clearing the dinner plates. You didn't have to twist Mr. Larkin's arm for the Grand Marnier and Jerry settled for a suggested cappuccino. The hostess stopped and asked how their dinner had been.

The waiter left the tab, invited them back, took eight steps and turned to see Mr. Larkin insisting that they use his credit card to pay. The waiter reconciled the tab immediately, thanking both men by name. Mr. Larkin left him a $20 tip **and** his business card. *"If you're ever looking for another sales job, son,"* Larkin said, *"Give us a call."*

The smiling hostess walked ahead of them and held the door open, quickly picking up a mint wrapper that had been lying on the floor. *"Goodnight Mr. Mathers, Mr. Larkin. Come back and see us again!"* the manager called out, waving at them from the middle of the dining room where she was talking to two other guests.

Our story has a happy ending. Jerry got the promotion. Sam was sent to a week-long seminar on "Service Awareness" in Fargo, North Dakota. Mr. Larkin issued a company-wide memo explaining that under no circumstances were clients of the Acme Widget Company ever to be wined, dined or entertained on the premises of the Hillside Restaurant at the risk of losing their clients. He would not approve company funds to reimburse any transgressors. The Valley View was recommended for all employees and clients. The moral?
Bad service happens all by itself. Good service has to be managed!

Putting it all together:
Managing our cycle of service

Don't let Sam's sad fate befall **your** guests. Service is our invisible product and obviously it involves a little more than sloganeering, smile training and serving hot food hot and cold food cold.

When someone gets bad service in your restaurant, the word can spread like wildfire. We're certain that you're insured against fire in your restaurant but are you insured against BAD SERVICE?

Since what "good service" is varies so much between each server and each guest, we'd like to suggest a solution to the "service" puzzle. It involves breaking down every facet or experience of the guest's visit into a separate unit, or contact point or "moment-of-truth," and then delineating:

1. How the customer **should** be treated to ensure 100 percent guest satisfaction.

2. Identifying which employees and managers interact with the guest at each customer contact point and will therefore have the greatest impact on the guest's experience.

3. Deciding on what training is necessary to ensure that each interaction or customer contact point results in a positive experience for the guest.

If you use a full-service restaurant as a model, you can break down your individual "Customer Contact Points" into twelve specific areas. By knowing what your service challenges are in each area, you know what you have to manage and who's responsible for the service delivery. String them all together in chronological order and they add up to hospitality's "Cycle of Service..."

#1   The Initial Contact

Guests can both make contact and form impressions of your restaurant, bar, or hotel's service *long* before they ever enter your establishment. How? By reading ads, hearing word-of-mouth "testimonials," driving by, walking by or calling on the phone. Of these three areas, the one we can best manage through better training is our phone manners. How and who should be taught these

▼   ▼   ▼   ▼

Cycle of Service

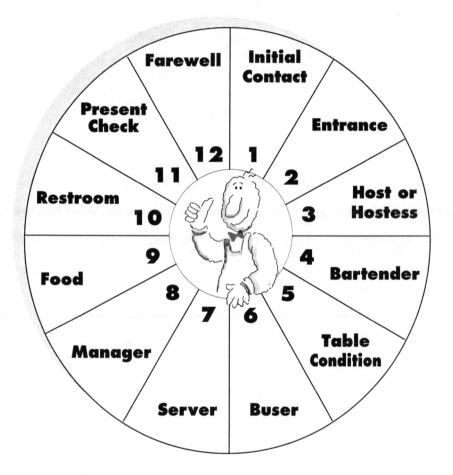

"*The most expensive thing in a restaurant is an empty chair!*"

— *Cris Roshko*

manners? That depends. Who answers the phone in your restaurant? Everyone who does should be trained in the behavior necessary to make the guest feel well served over the phone. Here are the areas you'll have to consider:

❖ Can your phone-answerers give accurate directions to your restaurant from other parts of town (airports, hotels, etcetera)? Determine the top five areas the majority of customers will ask directions from. Post the directions next to all your phones.

❖ Is your staff trained to smile when they answer the phone? (It makes the voice sound more pleasant.)

❖ If the caller must be put on hold, is the staff taught to check back within 30 seconds? Consider contracting with a service that will advertise your operation's menu, events or catering in a recording rather than subjecting the guest to "elevator-music."

❖ Never, *ever* let your staff say, *"It's really busy — can you call back???"* Why would the guest want to experience, in person, the indifference being shown over the phone?

❖ Is the staff knowledgeable about operating hours? Upcoming promotions? Parking? Special events? Entertainment? Cover charge? How to describe your food and operation?

Tip:
Phone your restaurant occasionally as a "mystery caller" and ask some of the questions above to gauge your staff's phone service. (For instance, call and ask, *"Is it busy?"* You may be surprised at what you'll hear.)

▼   ▼   ▼   ▼

Schedule training on proper phone manners for the entire staff at an employee meeting. Follow up during each floor shift to make sure it's being used.

#2   The Entrance Area

Author Karl Albrecht asks, "Have you ever been on an airplane, folded down the seat-back tray and noticed coffee stains on it that were never cleaned up? Doesn't that make you wonder how the airline services the parts of the plane that you *don't* see? Like the engines?" Of course it does; *that's* human nature. Well, our restaurant guests have the same "nature," and when they see:

❖ Beer bottles in your parking lot

❖ A burned out light bulb in front of your sign or entranceway

   ❖ A napkin, toothpick wrapper or any debris (leaves, dirt, etcetera) on the foyer floor

   ❖ Cigarette butts or paper lying on the sidewalk out front or in the planter boxes outside

   ❖ A stain or spill on the sidewalk by the front door

      ❖ Trash or grease alongside the dumpster

      ❖ Water dripping from leaky gutters

      ❖ Doors that stick

      ❖ A promotional sign or poster advertising an event that transpired a month ago

Our guests start forming impressions about how clean the areas are that you **don't** let them see, like the kitchen!

Tip:
Before — and during — every shift, managers and employees should inspect and **clean** the parking lot, foyer, planters, etcetera. This is a critical "Customer Contact Point." Some guests will never enter your front door if they get the impression outside that you're a poor housekeeper.

#3　The Host or Hostess Area

If we had it our way, we'd demolish every "host stand" in America's restaurants. Why? Because all too often, restaurateurs allow their host staff to hide behind these fancy podiums, forcing guests to open the front door themselves and approach the host or hostess to be "formally" greeted instead of vice versa. We see the host or hostess solidly entrenched behind the safety of the podium, like the Queen of Sheeba, beckoning the guests forward with a "*Smoking or non? Two for lunch? This way!*" And — whoosh — like a flash, they're gone, leaving the puzzled guests standing before the podium wondering where the hostess went and marvelling at the speed in which she left there.

The host or hostess is the first employee — and salesperson — that your guests meet. You never get a second chance to make a good impression. Here's what you should be training your host staff to do:

❖ Open the door for every guest that you can (both entering and exiting customers).

❖ Greet or acknowledge ("I'll be right with you!") all guests **by name** whenever possible within 30 seconds of their entrance.

Here are six ways to learn, remember and use guest's names:

1. Repeat their name aloud immediately after meeting them.

2. Say (or spell) the name silently three times to yourself. *Hint: Don't move your lips.*

3. Use the name aloud immediately.

4. Write it down on a business card or in a journal.

5. Introduce the person to someone else either directly or indirectly.

6. Ask them what they do. It's easier to remember a name associated with a profession.

❖ The "Please Wait To Be Seated" sign creates anxiety when the host staff isn't present. Teach your *servers* to look for and then acknowledge every waiting guest with a smile and a *"Hi! The hostess will be right with you!"* if he or she is off seating other guests. Make every customer feel wanted and appreciated the minute they set foot in your front door.

❖ If there is a waiting list, teach your host staff to "sell" the wait, rather than "challenge" the guest. A waiting guest experiences high anxiety. For instance, if there's a 20-minute wait, the host or hostess has two options of how he or she could inform the guest:

Wrong
"Four for dinner? There is a twenty-minute wait!"
Translation: "Your move!"

Right
*"Four for dinner? Great! Name please? Where would you like to sit Mr. Johnson? No problem, I can take care of that for you. There is a **short** twenty-minute wait, but if you'd like to have a seat at the bar I'll come get you the **minute***

your table is ready. The bartender can set you up with one of our great appetizers or specialty drinks!" Translation: "I know you hate to wait, but I'll do everything I can to make that wait as short as possible. I'm happy you're here!"

❖ When you take a reservation or add a name to the waiting list, train your host staff to *use that name:* "Mr. Johnson, your table is ready!" and "Enjoy your lunch, Mr. Johnson."

❖ Teach your host staff to carry the guests' drinks to the table, hang up their coats and pull out their chairs.

❖ Host staff should recommend **specific** food or beverage choices when seating their guests: "The nachos are great and the Irish Coffees are really popular. Enjoy your lunch/dinner!"

❖ **Never ignore departing guests!** Hold doors open for them, say good-bye and thank you. This is the number-one service blemish we note whenever we do "mystery" service audits for our clients. (See #12, page 137.)

❖ Make sure your host staff remembers to transfer the bar tab where appropriate.

Tip:
Get host staff together for a meeting and have them list all the service "extras" they can do for entering guests (such as opening doors, using names, picking up debris, pulling out chairs, etcetera). Now, role play those situations with **every** host and hostess, especially name usage. Remember, well-done is better than well-said. P.S. Consider offering a one dollar bonus for every new guest name that each host or hostess learns and uses.

▼   ▼   ▼   ▼

#4   The Cocktail Server or Bartender

Okay, let's assume that our VIP's (very important pocketbooks) have decided to wait at the bar or in the bar area until a table is ready. This can be a critical "Customer Contact Point." (Remember Jerry and Joan's experience?) The fact that our guests have to wait is already creating an anxious feeling, so it's critical that the cocktail server or bartender acknowledges those guests quickly and in a friendly manner. Here's what to train your cocktail and bar staff to do to ensure that a waiting guest is a happy guest:

❖ Acknowledge, greet and take each guest's drink order within two minutes.

❖ Deliver the drinks in less than **five** minutes.

❖ Hand the appetizer or "munchie" list to the guest. Suggest a choice of at least two *specific* appetizers. Recommend your favorite.

❖ Watch for bartenders suffering from the deadly "Sink Eye Syndrome" (washing glasses with eyes down), instead of acknowledging, serving and talking to new guests at the bar.

❖ Do your bartenders know the daily food and drink specials? Are they recommending them?

❖ Teach them to name premium beers *first and last* when the guest asks what kind of beers you have. (Remember primacy and recency.)

❖ Make sure bartenders or cocktail servers are not spending too much time talking with "regulars" or other employees at the bar when they could be talking to or serving new customers. *Today's "regulars" were yesterday's "unknowns!"*

❖ Are bartenders "upselling" liquor in every cocktail? (*"Would you like to try Bombay in that gin and tonic?"*)

❖ Are servers and bartenders learning and *using* guests' names?

❖ Check the overall appearance of the bar *and* the bartender: are they both neat, clean and uncluttered?

❖ **It's more fun to eat in a bar than it is to drink in a restaurant!** (Roberts' Law) Teach your bartenders to suggest lunch and dinner at the bar to all their waiting guests when appropriate.

#5   The Table

Okay, so our guests are finally led to their table. Now a whole new set of service considerations arise in our VIPs relative to this piece of furniture:

❖ Is the table steady or rocking and rolling? Use the "Universal Restaurant Table Stabilizer" (U.R.T.S.): a matchbook.

❖ Are the menus clean and free of spots? If not, clean them immediately or toss them out. Make sure that the lunch menus are out at lunch and the dinner menus are out at dinner.

❖ Are the table tents clean and in place? If not, wipe or toss them.

▼   ▼   ▼   ▼

❖ Have the dust, crumbs and stains been cleaned off the tables and chairs?

❖ Have the tabletop condiments (like salt and pepper shakers) been wiped clean? Or did the last guest eating ribs, chicken or french fries use the salt shaker *before* they used the napkin?

#6   The Buser or Service Assistant

Now our guests are sitting at a table with clean condiments and spotless menus. Their next experience is most likely with the buser who arrives to remove extra place settings or pour water. What impression is the guest getting here? Are the busers smiling, friendly? Or do they look as if they just killed their parents? Busers must be taught to:

❖ Quietly and *carefully* remove dirty dishware, flatware and glasses from tables. Role play with your busers how to correctly do this. They have a huge impact on controlling the cost of physical inventory and breakage.

❖ Your buser should also know your restaurant's food and beverage items as well as a server does (everyone who works for you should be thought of, and managed as, a salesperson).

❖ Busers should also be taught to respond properly to commonly asked guest questions:

1. Question: *"Where's the cigarette machine?"*
Response: *"What kind do you smoke? I'll be happy to get you a pack!"*

2. Question: *"Where's the bathroom?"*
Response: *"I'll show you."* Lead them part way if necessary. Don't just jerk your thumb like you're hitchhiking through the dining room.

Important: This question indicates that the guest is a first-time visitor to your restaurant. Alert a manager and do something special for the new customer.

❖ Check busers' appearances. Are they bathed? Neat? Are their uniforms clean? Are their bar rags rinsed?

Your busers are likely to be asked more questions by your guest than any other employee. Make sure you train them to know the answers.

#7   The Server

Servers spend more time with your guests than any other member of your staff. What do they need to do to create a positive service experience for everyone they wait on? They could read this book for starters, and then:

❖ Know everything on the menu in terms of what's in it and, also, what would go well with it.

❖ Acknowledge and greet each guest quickly, *no longer* than two minutes after they've been seated.

❖ Suggest premium liquor in all cocktails. It makes the drink taste better, servers are tipped more and when the guest drinks better, the server drinks better!

❖ Suggest *specific* appetizers before you leave the table to get their first drinks. It saves you time and steps.

❖ Get your guests' first drinks to them *no longer* than five minutes after taking the order.

❖ *Learn* and *use* guests' names.

▼   ▼   ▼   ▼

❖ Make specific suggestions at **every** step of the meal: drinks, appetizers, sides, wine, desserts, after-dinner drinks.

❖ Check your employees' appearances. Are uniforms clean? Is hair combed? Is perfume, makeup or cologne appropriate or overbearing? Are there food stains on aprons?

❖ Use your daily team meetings as an opportunity to inspect the appearance and "combat readiness" of your "troops" by quizzing them on product knowledge and sales dialogue. Remember: **You get what you inspect, not what you expect.**

#8   The Manager

Demonstrating management presence to your guests is a critical "Customer Contact Point." You can't manage a restaurant from a perch on a barstool or from an office in the back. Don't "manage the floor," *work the room.* Try to greet every guest in your dining room or bar. Watch your guests' faces as they receive their food. Make eye contact. Smile. Introduce yourself and learn your guests' names. (You may want to start a journal of guests' names to help you remember them the next time they come in.) It sets an example for the rest of the staff. Find out where your customers work, how business is, where they're from and what their hobbies are. Make suggestions to the guests yourself , *"Our pie tonight is homemade blueberry. Make sure you save some room for it!"* Exchange business cards when appropriate. (See page 142 for Ten Skills Every Effective Restaurant Manager Must Master.)

Oh, yeah. **And never, EVER, point in a dining room.** At anybody or anything. Thank you.

#9 The Food

So far, we've managed all the "Customer Contact Points" positively. Now it's time for the moment the guest has been waiting for: the food. How long did it take to get there? It's a restaurant rule that *"unoccupied time passes slower than occupied time,"* which is another good reason to suggest appetizers: they fill up the "dead time" between entree ordering and delivery with server-suggested munchies. What does the food look like? Is that the way it's *supposed* to look? Is it garnished properly? Have the necessary condiments (ketchup, mustard, mayonaise, crackers, more napkins, etcetera) been delivered? Great! Now be sure that servers or bartenders check back within *two bites* (not "two minutes") to be certain that the food tastes the way the *guest* expected it to. Observe your guests' faces as they look at and taste their food. What do their expressions tell you? Role play with your servers how to positively handle a guest complaint relative to a problem with food or beverage.

#10 The Bathroom

Sometime after eating, many guests will now visit your bathroom. Does it look like your bathroom at home would look if you were throwing a dinner party? Make sure that managers and staff routinely check the bathroom throughout the shift and clean up water around the sinks and paper on the floor and report any plumbing problems. (This will take some training; most employees won't report problems in the bathroom if they know they'll be asked to rectify them!)

#11　The Check Presentation and Check Reconciliation

There's a funny habit restaurant customers have. They'll sit leisurely at lunch or dinner, sometimes for hours, *but once they've decided to leave, they get in a hurry to go.* This step (#11) is an extremely important "Customer Contact Point." You can effectively manage the previous ten steps and then blow it all by taking too long to deliver the tab or — worse yet — taking too long to reconcile it with the guest's credit card, cash or check. (This can be especially deadly in the Twilight Zone of many restaurants: between the hours of 2 p.m. and 5 p.m.). Most servers realize it's important to drop the check, but then they saunter off to do their side work, forgetting to check and see if the guest is ready to pay. How many times have you seen a guest with their tab and cash or credit card in hand walk up to someone in your restaurant (other than their server) and ask for help reconciling it? Teach your servers to walk no more than *eight steps* away from their tables after dropping the check and turn and see if the guest has put down money for it. **Remember: This is the point at which the guest is deciding the server's tip!** A bad impression here can undo all the previous good impressions. Teach your waitstaff to always drop the check and reconcile it when the guest is ready, not when it's "convenient" for the server.

#12　The Farewell

We have four distinct objectives with every departing guest:

1. To make sure their experience in our restaurant was pleasurable.
2. To thank them for their patronage — by *name.*
3. To invite them back for another visit soon.
4. To make sure their last impression is a positive one.

Host staff, servers, busers and managers all have the responsibility to bid our departing guests farewell. But host staff and managers usually have the most frequent opportunities to do so. Here's the behavior associated with a farewell that's guaranteed to generate a repeat visit:

❖ Help guests on with their jackets or coats.

❖ Open the door for every departing guest.

❖ Thank guests by name and invite them back for a specific occasion: *"Come back and check out our Sunday brunch!"*

❖ It takes only a fleeting moment to wrap and deliver it, but the memory of it can last a lifetime. It's the only thing people can wear that never goes out of style. And one size fits everyone. It's called a **smile.**.

None of us is as important as all of us.

▼   ▼   ▼   ▼

❖ SMILE! SMILE! SMILE! When you smile at departing guests, they smile back. Arriving guests then see departing guests leaving with a smile. That says to them *"Hey, these guys just had a great time here ... I can't wait!"*

These twelve "Customer Contact Points" of service excellence are your road map to success in this business. Teach these dozen steps of service satisfaction to your staff and you'll see your external and internal marketing efforts rewarded. Ignore them, and your marketing problems won't go away. But your customers might.

A quick word on teamwork

Managing our customer contact points is the strongest argument there is for teamwork in our business. None of us is as important as all of us. As Emerson pointed out, "No member of a crew is praised for the rugged individualism of his rowing." In a related vein, Harvey Mackay points out that "the boat won't go unless we all row!" At regularly scheduled employee meetings always recognize and reward accomplishments from every department. Allow ten minutes of "complaint time." These steps help to foster collaboration and build teams.

The twelve "Customer Contact Points" we just analyzed are based on a full-service restaurant. Depending on your type of operation, the points may vary somewhat. For example, a restaurant with valet parking or a drive-thru window would have several other points to consider. Use the following action plan to determine *your* restaurant's "moments-of-truth."

● ●

"Treat guests the way they want to be treated, not the way you want to be treated."

— *Jim Cathcart*

● ●

Action plan for defining the customer contact points in your restaurant

1. Have your entire waitstaff read this section of *Service That Sells!*

2. Call your service staff together for an employee meeting.

3. Explain the twelve "Customer Contact Points."

4. Break the group into teams with an employee from each department. Give each team a piece of flip chart paper and marking pen.

5. Give them 15 to 20 minutes to define the number of "Customer Contact Points" in your restaurant and write them down on the flip chart paper.

6. Choose a leader for each group to come up front, post their "Customer Contact Points" and explain why they chose them.

7. Review all the group's "Customer Contact Points" and decide — as a group — which ones are necessary to better manage service and sales in your restaurant.

8. Discuss what contribution each department can make to manage each "Customer Contact Point" to give guests a better experience.

▼   ▼   ▼   ▼

The Theatre
A day in the life of a restaurant manager: Another opening, another show!

What is the foodservice manager's role in the operation of a prosperous restaurant? After more than 25 years in this business we've come to the conclusion that we're in **show business** every day. Not Hollywood-style exactly, but closer in spirit to New York's Broadway.

An effective restaurant manager is like the writer, producer and director of a high budget Broadway show. You must audition, rehearse and cast both the "actors" (front of the house) and the "technicians" (heart of the house). You may have to rewrite the "script" (service and sales focus) — daily — to accommodate the ever-changing elements of the cast, crew, theater and even the audience.

You have to coach and direct all of the actors and actresses (lead roles *and* "bit" players) in both their lines and actions. You have to help them understand what their "motivation" is, how to play the role and how to act to get the desired result from the audience (your customers). The successful producer-director does not set the lights or microphones him or herself, but shows the technical crew how, and then rehearses with them as much as with the "players."

Rehearsal schedules, like training sessions, are routinely set, scene by scene, act by act, until the entire play is memorized by the player and every light and sound cue is mastered by the technicians to coincide perfectly with the actions of the cast. Why? So that the audience will be thrilled by the performance and want to see it over and over again.

Costumes (uniforms) are prepared and worn, the props (table tents, wine lists, menus) are put in place. And as dress rehearsals begin, both costumes and props start to bring the action to life. "Make believe" begins to evolve into reality.

Every time you unlock the front door of your restaurant, it's "opening night." Maybe you'll play to SRO crowds and maybe your "theatre" will entertain only a half-full house. Unfortunately, some nights you may be completely dark. It doesn't depend on "ticket" sales. *It depends on the audience buying tickets.* You can't play very well to empty seats.

Are the actors saying the right words? Do they need prompting? Are they using all their props? Are the technicians producing the necessary light, sound and color? The way you — and they — rehearsed it? Most importantly, is the producer-director there, nightly, in the wings? Encouraging, cheerleading and coaching award-winning performances from each and every member of the cast and crew each and every time the curtain goes up? If not, it's wise to remember that your audience will hold the writer-director-producer (not the actors or technicians) responsible when a show bombs. This is show biz folks. So put on a happy face.

'Nuff said. You can have the best show in town. But if you can't sell it, you still got it!

▼   ▼   ▼   ▼

Ten skills every effective restaurant manager must master

1. **Master the art of public speaking.**
    Communication skills are your number-one asset in this industry. The better you can organize and articulate your thoughts, the better you can talk to guests, negotiate with vendors and supervise your staff. Attend Toastmasters, videotape your employee meetings and volunteer to address your restaurant association or church group. Being a better speaker not only builds confidence, it also enhances your leadership perception among the staff.

2. **Plan your work, then work your plan.**
    Don't try to manage "time." It's a dimension, not a thing. Instead, manage activities. Every night *before* you leave work, write down and prioritize the **six most important things** you have to do the next day. Then do those things in order of priority. Making this a nightly habit will be your lifelong friend.

3. **See training as a philosophy, not a department.**
    The primary goal of every manager should be to teach everyone on the staff something new every day. When we teach, we learn twice. If you think training is expensive, try ignorance.

4. **Market your restaurant, don't "manage" it.**
    The following is a good story illustrating this point:
    > Two hikers encountered an angry bear in the forest. One of the men opened up his knapsack, pulled out his running shoes and began putting them on as fast as he could. The other watched and said incredulously, "You don't think you're going to outrun that bear, do you?"

▼ ▼ ▼ ▼

"I don't have to outrun the bear," the first man replied. "I only have to outrun you."

Whom do we outrun? Our competition. Excel at the art of "local store" or neighborhood marketing. National Restaurant Association studies show that over 70 percent of a restaurant's customer base comes from within a four-mile radius of its property. If you could get every current customer to return one more time per month, it means your gross sales will double ... without spending one cent on advertising. So what are you doing to market to your neighbors? We recommend getting to know them and getting to know all about them. Join local business and neighborhood associations or even church groups. Consider implementing Frequent Diner programs. Stop by *every* table to say hello, learn something about every guest. Buy them a dessert and encourage a feeling of reciprocity. ("We'll be back!")

5. **Learn, remember and use the guest's names.** Three ways to get better at it: first, *listen* when they introduce themselves. Second, repeat the name aloud and use it at least three times during the conversation. Finally, write the name down on a sheet of paper or on the back of their business card. It helps memory retention when you put their name in your handwriting.

6. **Treat employees like internal customers.** Managers are rewarded not for what they do, but for what their people do, and the way you treat your employees determines the way they'll treat your guests. Welcome them with a smile and a kind word when they get to work, not "Hurry up, we're getting slammed!" Create an opportunity for them to critique the managers anonymously in writing. It's been said that if you're not serving the guest directly, you'd better be serving some-

one who is. But we like to say that you're hired by the people you report to and fired by the people who report to you. Be a leader, not a boss.

7. Never lose your showbiz face at work.
What if there was a video camera in your restaurant's dining room, bar and kitchen that was always trained on you? When you're "onstage," which is anywhere in view of your guests or employees, what expressions are you sporting? Do you always appear content, smiling and in control? Or do you sometimes sport an expression resembling a *pit bull on crack?* Be like a duck: keep calm and unruffled on the surface but paddle like the devil underneath!

8. Manage your personal income.
We restaurant managers are notorious for *not* being very good stewards of our income. Seek professional money management advice and invest safely and wisely. How many times have you run out of *month* before the end of your *money??* A dollar saved is a dollar earned. A dollar well-managed is a dollar oft-multiplied!

9. Manage your health.
Not many jobs are more time-consuming and stress-producing than restaurant management. You're not getting any younger, but you can stay healthier by spending more time with your family, watching your diet and working in a little more exercise. Watch out for too many C.A.T.S. (caffeine, alcohol, tobacco, salt and sugar). Life: can't live with it, can't live without it.

10. Remember that good enough never is.
Invest in your own future by turning your car into a mobile university with educational audiotapes. Attend seminars at your restaurant association trade shows or sign up for business skills seminars

offered through private companies. Read books on service, sales, management and training. Remember: if you always do what you always did, you always *get* what you always *got!*

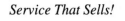

COURSE 7: A Little Nightcap
Service That Sells! summary

Just do it!!

We hope we've provided you with a lot of good ideas in this book. But now, where do you start? The answer is: at the beginning. But don't just *talk* about it. **Do it.**

You *can* improve your service, acquire more customers and make more money without having to put in any more time in your restaurant or bar by simply remembering that **To sell is to serve.** Implement the ideas in this book that you feel are most relevant to your operation. Try one a day.

• •

"It is no profit to learn well if
you neglect to do well."
— *Jim Buelt*

• •

Or one a week. **But do something!** We suggest that you assign *Service That Sells!* to every manager in your operation. Ask them to list (in writing) the 15 best ideas they got from this book. Then schedule a meeting to discuss and list their ideas. Now prioritize their list with a timetable and deadlines for implementation. Assign a specific manager to be the "captain" responsible for seeing each idea or project through. Then, assign chapters three and four to your servers. Ask each one to compile a written book report listing the ten best ideas they got from the text. At your next staff meeting, break them into groups with their lists and have them prioritize the top ten. As we said earlier, solve problems by getting your people involved in the solution.

Remember that getting started is often the hardest part of a job. We sometimes need all of our energy just for starting. We're like cars — only a small

▼   ▼   ▼   ▼

percentage of an engine's power is necessary to run an automobile, but all its power may be necessary to start it.

It took us a long time, a lot of mistakes and a wealth of commitment to make the *Service That Sells!* program work in our own stores, but it has paid for itself a hundred times over.

How much? An average **increase of $200,000 in gross sales per year per restaurant** without raising menu prices or spending one more penny in advertising. That $200,000 a year is the result of merely raising our guest checks one dollar per person. What can you teach your staff to sell more of each day? Sixty more sides of french fries? Fourteen more appetizers? Three more bottles of wine? Twenty-seven more cups of soup? Fifty-seven more premium cocktails? It honestly is not that difficult. Train your servers to sell and your sellers to serve. Service is love in work clothes, they say.

The restaurant business is like a daily hundred-yard dash with opening the front door being the "starting gun" and closing it the "tape." Read this book, assign your staff to read this book, and *use* the information. You'll win the race every day.

Thanks for sticking with us this far. If you'd like more information about our company, or if you'd like to chat about your service and sales challenges and how this program can work in your operation, call or write us at Pencom, P.O. Box 1920, Denver, CO 80201, (303) 595-3991.

Now, we'd like to leave you with the following 15 thoughts:

1. **Always invest in your greatest resource, your employees.**
   Like the Japanese proverb says: If he works for you, you work for him. Love 'em and lead 'em.

2. **Remember, the person on top of the mountain didn't fall there.**
   Improve your service. Raise those sales. Make it happen. Like Johnny Sain once said, *"Don't tell me about the labor pains, show me the baby!"*

3. **Success isn't how far you've gotten, it's the distance you traveled from where you started.**
   Be patient but persistent with sales training. Fall seven times, stand up eight.

4. **The reason a lot of people do not recognize an opportunity when they meet it** is that it usually goes around wearing overalls and looking like hard work. So it is with sales and service training.

5. **Nothing lasts as long as a box of cereal you don't like and an employee meeting you can't stand.**
   Make your training fun, lively and relevant.

6. **People would rather agree than obey.**
   Show your staff *why* better service, higher sales and lower costs are essential. When your restaurant succeeds, *they* succeed.

7. **In every service opportunity, there is a sales opportunity.**
   And in every sales opportunity, there is a service opportunity.

8. **In baseball, a game won today will count as much as a game won at the end of the season,**

▼   ▼   ▼   ▼

as far as the averages go. So it is with the hospitality business — *every day's a new game.*

9. **Never resent problems at work.**
Experience comes from learning what to do when something goes wrong.

10. **You don't have to be sick to get better.**
When is the last time your guests got too much *good* service? When is the last time you made too much money?

11. **Of all the people who will never leave you, you're the only one.** The best way to retain quality help is to create an environment they don't want to leave. We do that by treating our staff as internal customers and leading, not managing, them to achieve their potential — and have fun — everyday.

"If you can see the light at the end of the tunnel, you're looking the wrong way."

— *Barry Commoner*

12. **The answer is "YES!" What was the question?**
This is the standard response every service-driven company must learn when our customers request anything.

13. **The will to win is not nearly as important as the will to *prepare* to win.**

14. **We are the only business whose assets walk out the front door everyday!**

15. **And last, but not least, remember: This is the hospitality business, show business ... *have fun, not a heart attack!***

If you always do *what you always* did, *you always* get *what you always* got!

Appendix
Service That Sells!

**101 Ways to Sell More
Beer ◆ Appetizers ◆ Sides ◆ Desserts ◆
Wine ◆ Specialty Drinks**

Ten ways to sell more beer:

1. Use colorful table tents on every table and at every other bar stool that feature and highlight the beers you offer.

2. Teach host staff to mention beer when they seat customers, such as, *"Our appetizers are listed here and we feature Bud and Bud Light on tap!"*

3. Sell bottled beer by "the bucket" at a special price.

"I think there are other types of table tents, don't you?"

4. Sell a "bucket of ice" for $8 and include four "complimentary" bottles of beer.

5. List beers brewed in the United States as "American" beers, not "domestic" beers. It sounds better.

6. Train servers and bartenders to suggest beer as part of their opening dialogue: *"Can I get you something to drink to start ... a cold Molson, Sam Adams or Bud Dry?"*

7. If you offer pitchers of draft beer, train your servers to always suggest a trade-up to a pitcher when two or more customers at the same table ask for a draft.

8. Pair up beers with specific appetizers at a special price, for example, *"A pitcher of Miller Lite and nachos only $6.95!"* List the pairs on your menu or on table tents and train servers and hostesses to point them out to guests.

9. Keep bottles of your beer selection prominently displayed (and dust-free) on the back bar.

10. When guests request water, coffee or tea, train your servers to ask if they'd like to try a non-alcohol brew: *"Have you ever tried O'Doul's? It's a great non-alcohol brew from Bud. They're on special today for only $2."*

Ten ways to sell more appetizers:

1. Have your appetizers listed separately on a table tent or table card (in addition to listing them on your menu) and place them on every table and at the bar. List your wines by the glass or desserts on the other side of the table tent.

2. Have host staff always recommend at least two of your appetizers, by name, to every guest they seat. Practice this dialogue every day with your host staff.

3. Combine appetizers with glasses of wine at a lower price than if you bought each separately. Highlight the pairing by "boxing" them on your menu.

4. Offer bite-sized "samples" of your appetizers (with a verbal description of what they are) to guests waiting for lunch or dinner during your busy periods.

5. Train your servers to suggest appetizers immediately after taking their guest's first drink order.

6. Have an appetizer list in front of every other seat at the bar. Train your bartenders to consistently suggest appetizers with every drink order.

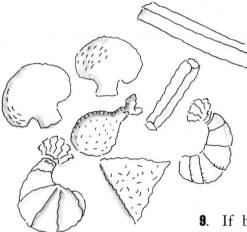

7. Offer a sampler platter of your most popular appetizers on your menu at a special price so guests can graze on each.

8. Offer "samples" of your appetizers to people seated at the bar. They'll soon request a full order.

9. If bar patrons decline the bartender's appetizer suggestion, teach your bartenders to ask again after the second or third drink.

10. "Box" your best dollar-margin appetizers on your menu to draw more attention to them as guests' eyes scan the menu.

Forty-three ways to sell more wine:

1. Suggest wine at three different times:
   - Initial greeting
   - When taking the entree order or right after turning it in
   - During the "dessert zone" (suggest sparkling wines, cabernet sauvignon, port, etcetera.)

2. Mention wine twice in your opening dialogue to newly seated guests: *"Can I get you something to drink?* (pause) *A glass of wine, a beer or a cocktail? Our featured wine today is the Sutter Home Chardonnay."* Studies show that guests will remember the first and last thing you say.

3. If you want servers to know your wine list well, make it as simple as possible relative to your menu.

4. List complementary wines after each food item on your menu.

5. Have servers wear buttons promoting a particular wine (call your local distributor).

6. List your wines on the back page of your menu so that each guest sees a wine list when looking at a companion's menu.

7. If guests decline a server's wine suggestion during the initial greeting, don't forget to suggest it again when they order entrees. Many guests prefer cocktails to start and then wine with the "main" course.

8. Let your staff taste the incredible sensation of a dry red cabernet sauvignon with any of your chocolate desserts. *"It's like fireworks for your tastebuds!"* Have them suggest a glass with every chocolate dessert.

9. List wines by the glass or featured wines on table tents and place them on every table and at every other seat at the bar.

10. The number-one reason servers don't suggest wine is because they might sell it and have to open it! Let servers practice daily by opening house wine bottles for the bartender, or practice opening "dummy" bottles that your wine vendor can supply.

11. Make sure that every server or bartender has a wine opener with them on every shift. Inspect daily!

12. Assign each server and bartender specific daily wine sales goals before each shift. Reward achievers with a draw from a bowl of $1 state lottery tickets.

13. Have monthly product knowledge training sessions on your wines. Include tasting the wines combined with bite-sized samples of your menu items. *Test* your waitstaff immediately with a quiz. (Consider having one of your wine representatives sponsor and lead these sessions.)

14. Contact your wine vendors to provide merchandise (t-shirts, wine, glasses, racks, key chains, etcetera) for a month-long wine sales contest. (Be sure to check your state laws first.)

15. Suggest port wine with any dessert that features nuts (especially walnuts or hazelnuts). It's an incredible taste sensation!

16. Have servers recommend their favorite wine as a "featured" wine. This doesn't mean you have to discount the price; it just means the server is featuring the wine.

17. Send regular customers a birthday or anniversary card good for a free glass or bottle of wine.

18. List your wines from driest (at the top of the list) to sweetest (at bottom). They will be easier for your servers to remember and suggest. Indicate this on the menu so guests know, too.

19. If you routinely provide incentives for wine sales, consider doubling the incentive at lunch since it's usually harder to sell wine then.

20. Cut out pictures of a variety of different-looking people from magazines or ads. At a server meeting, distribute the pictures and ask the server to tell you what specific wine or wines they'd suggest to that person. This is a great exercise for confronting the stereotypes some servers have that certain customers "don't look like" they want wine.

21. Show photos of a variety of your menu items and quiz servers to say which wines they'd pair up and suggest with that food.

22. Offer "passports" to your customers to encourage them to try all of your wines from around the world. (It works great, just like a "beer club")!

23. When two guests order a glass of the same wine, train servers to say, "If you think you'll be having more than one glass, you may want to consider a bottle. You'll each get several glasses and save a few dollars."

24. Point out to servers that selling a bottle of wine to a table saves steps to and from the bar as opposed to having to go back and forth each time the guests order a glass.

25. Teach servers to always suggest mid-priced wines to guests unless they specifically ask for a premium vintage. This builds customer confidence.

26. When guests decline dessert suggestions, recommend a glass of champagne or port wine.

27. Train servers to suggest a bottle of champagne to any group (from two to two hundred) that is celebrating anything (birthday, promotion, moving, winning a tournament, new hair style, you name it!).

28. Point out to servers that selling bottles of wine is the quickest route to higher tips.

29. Always suggest a bottle of wine first. If guests decline, suggest a split. If they decline the split, recommend a glass. (Two steps forward, one step back.) Do not use the term

"split" with customers — instead say something like, "cute little half bottle."

30. Get your restaurant's "resident wine expert" from the local radio talk show to promote wine knowledge (and your restaurant).

31. Display bottles of wine on each table with a card that describes that wine, what kind of food it complements and the price. (See if you can get sealed and water-filled bottles or empty versions from the distributor so theft won't be a problem.)

32. Consider putting wine glasses on every table. If guests decline a wine suggestion, remove the glasses.

33. Design weekly or monthly promotions that feature pairings of wine and food specials from a specific country.

34. Train hostesses to point out wine lists as they seat each guest. Practice this with them daily.

35. Never let servers say, *"Do you want some wine?"* Instead, have them say, *"Have you had a chance to look over our wine list? We've got a great selection.* (Pause). *Do you prefer red or white?* (Wait for response). *Sweet or dry?* (Wait for response). *Well then, let me recommend the _____ or _____."*

WINES FROM AROUND THE WORLD

▼   ▼   ▼   ▼

36. Train servers to nod their head as they suggest wine. This subtle body language (the "Sullivan Nod") helps guests agree with your recommendation.

37. To sell second bottles of wine, pour out the remainder of the first bottle into the most empty glasses (ladies first) and then say, *"Can I bring you another bottle of Cabernet Now, or should I wait until I bring your entrees?"* Assume the sale!

38. Set daily and weekly wine sales goals for managers. This encourages server coaching.

39. Create an incentive or bonus system for managers who exceed those goals.

40. Write a column about wine in your local restaurant association newsletter or, better yet, your local newspaper.

41. Train servers to master the simple etiquette of wine opening and pouring. Role play with each server until they can do it in their sleep.

42. Consider selling wine glasses imprinted with your logo at a special price if your customers buy a featured wine bottle.

43. Offer splits (half bottles) of wine or champagne. They're cute and they sell.

Six ways to sell more premium liquor in your cocktails:

1. Train your servers and bartenders to know at least two "call" liquors for each well drink: rum, tequila, bourbon, scotch, gin and vodka.

2. Test servers and bartenders daily with verbal quizzes on their premium liquor product knowledge.

3. Always offer a choice of at least two "call" brands when suggesting premium liquor.

4. Teach servers to say the word "try" when suggesting call liquor. For instance, *"Would you like to try Tanqueray or Bombay in your gin and tonic?"*

5. Have servers **nod** their head (subtle body language) as they say, *"Would you like to try Finlandia or Absolut in your martini?"*

6. Don't fall victim to the myth that "the bar makes more money from well than call drinks." This is wrong for two reasons:

a. You paid for that bottle of Bacardi Black, Cuervo Gold or Chivas already. It's sitting on your shelf. Sell it!

b. You're confusing "pour cost" (p.c.) with gross margin dollars. For example, let's assume that your "well" gin has a p.c. (pour cost) of 20 percent and that your "call" gin has a p.c. of 25 percent. You offer your well gin for $2 a drink, your call gin for $2.50. That $2 "well" has a gross margin of **$1.60** per drink. Now, that $2.50 "call" drink with a 25 percent p.c. costs you about 62¢ to pour, but it results in a gross margin of **$1.88** per drink. The "premium" drink results in a 15 percent higher gross margin than a "call" drink! Remind your servers that when the guest drinks better, the server drinks better, too.

Five ways to sell more "sides" with appetizers or entrees:

1. Train and quiz your staff daily to know at least two "sides" or "extras" to automatically suggest with your most popular appetizers or entrees. Play the product knowledge game known as "I say, you say":

Manager:	"Guest says, 'I'll have some potato skins.' *You* say?"
Server:	"Would you like to try guacamole or spiced chicken with that?"
Manager:	"Guest says 'I'll have the broiled sword-fish.' You say?"
Server:	"Good choice. Would you like to start with a cup of our famous clam chowder or French onion soup?"
Manager:	"Guest says 'New York strip.' You say?"
Server:	"Would you like to try grilled onions or sauteed mushrooms with that?"

2. Let staff "taste test" sides with appetizers or entrees (such as guacamole or ground beef on the potato skins) at training sessions before each shift.

3. List the prices of all "sides" on a sheet of paper. Post this sheet of prices in your training manuals and the server stations for easy reference. Test your staff thoroughly in writing and verbally every day.

4. Teach your servers to use the "Sullivan Nod" as they suggest sides.

5. List your "sides" and their prices on your menu, possibly right next to the food items.

Eleven ways to sell more desserts:

1. Teach servers to "plant the seed" for dessert sales at least twice before guests finish their meal: once when taking the entree order and again when you deliver the entree. Be spe-

cific in your suggestion: *"Be sure to save room for our deep dish apple pie or New York cheese-cake!"*

2. Train servers to **never** say *"Do you want some dessert?"* You're begging them to say "no"! Instead, train your servers to say: *"Now we're ready for the best part of the meal, one of our great desserts. The pie of the day is fresh-baked huckleberry with a cinnamon crust. We've got vanilla ice cream to go with it. And our chocolate mousse is to die for!"* Hear the difference?

3. Ask your servers to write down at least three descriptive adjectives or phrases for each dessert at a training meeting, then have them use those phrases in role-playing. Exchange descriptions and have them role-play again.

4. Use a dessert tray or cart.

5. Suggest that lunch guests take a dessert to go. It beats a Snickers bar from a candy machine at the 3 o'clock break.

6. Have an employee take free samplers of your desserts to local business offices between 1:15 and 1:30 p.m. Distribute them to the workers; don't leave them for the boss. (The workers are usually more frequent guests.)

7. Give guests who've waited too long for lunch or dinner a free dessert. They'll probably order one the next time they're in.

8. When guests hesitate at dessert suggestions, offer to bring them one dessert and several forks!

9. List your desserts on a table tent or separate menu in addition to your regular menu. Train your servers to use these "props" when suggesting desserts.

10. Train your servers to use the "Sullivan Nod" and say *"Coffee?"* with every dessert sale, but *only* after first suggesting liqueurs (if you serve liquor in your restaurant).

11. Teach your host staff to recommend during the seating dialogue that guests save room for a specific dessert.

Sixteen ways to sell more after dinner drinks:

1. Always suggest after-dinner drinks before saying *"coffee?"* Saying "coffee" signals the "end of the meal" for most guests.

2. Always suggest coffee as a companion drink after the guest orders liqueurs such as Grand Marnier, Sambuca, Bailey's, Cognac, brandy, etcetera.

3. If guests decline the server's suggestion of liqueurs or alcohol coffee drinks (such as Irish Coffee) train your servers to *nod* as they say, *"Four coffees?"* **Assume the sale.** (If you sell espresso or cappuccino, always suggest them before you suggest regular coffee.)

4. Consider using a "liqueur tray" of your most popular cordials to help sell after-dinner drinks. Use mini "airline" bottles in a small wooden rack that's easily held and displayed by the server. Fill these bottles with water to

control inventory, and pour from the big bottles at the bar, of course.

5. Display a list of your after-dinner drinks on a table tent or as a card inserted on the top of the salt and pepper caddy. Place them on all tables and in front of every other bar stool.

6. Train your servers to suggest hot specialty drinks, such as Cappuccino Sausalito and Keoke Coffee, when guests decline dessert.

7. Recommend a glass of red cabernet sauvignon with all chocolate desserts.

8. Recommend port wine with all desserts featuring nuts.

9. Do not offer after-dinner drinks with difficult recipes that take too much time or hassle for bartenders to make (for example, a peanut butter ice cream kahlua parfait). Bartenders may encourage your servers not to sell them.

10. Add a unique novelty garnish (paper palm trees, sunglasses, small rubber monkeys, etcetera) to certain house specialty after dinner drinks and increase the price.

11. Serve your specialty drinks in unusual glasses such as 20-inch-high sixteen-ounce glasses.

12. Don't make the names of your after dinner specialty drinks too unusual or servers will have difficulty remembering what's in each one.

13. The most popular alcohol coffee drinks in the U.S. are Irish Coffee, Keoke Coffee, Bailey's and coffee and Kahlua and Coffee. Always include these four drinks on your menu.

▼   ▼   ▼   ▼

14. Add dry ice to turn ho-hum drinks into **drama drinks.**

15. Train your servers and bartenders to know the recipe of every alcohol speciality drink and test them daily.

16. In a training meeting, let servers taste the hot drinks in combination with dessert samples. Ask them to describe the complementary flavors.

Taming the guest from hell

A customer in a side street beanery called his waitress over. "I'm ready to order," he barked. The waitress pulled out her guest check pad. "I want two pieces of whole grain wheat toast," the customer growled, "*not* cracked grain. The toast should be lightly tan, not dark. I want *one* strip of bacon — lean — not fatty, and done brown but not so brown that it's crisp. Then I want two eggs — fried so that the yolk is firm but not *too* firm. And I want the white part runny, but not *too* runny. I want the edges crisp, but not burnt. Is that clear?"

The waitress paused for a second and asked "Just one question, sir. The hen's name is Doris ... *will that be a problem?*"

▼　　▼　　▼　　▼

Thank You ...

for reading *Service That Sells!* If you like this book, be sure to catch our award-winning live seminars. Call up your local restaurant association and ask when they've scheduled their next Pencom seminar in *your* area.

Sex ...

is a word they say to use to get people to read a new paragraph, and apparently it works! If you have a service anecdote (good or bad) that you'd like to share with us or a service or sales related training tip you'd like your fellow restaurateurs to know about, please call:

1-800-247-8514

We'll send you a free "Day in the Life of a Restaurant Manager" poster for your effort and give you credit in our next book.

Thanks.

Notes

Now that you've read the book, why not ...

SEE THE SEMINAR

HEAR THE AUDIOTAPE

WATCH THE VIDEO

and simultaneously improve your profits, performance and productivity!

Here's how...

Award winning seminars

Best prices in the business! For detailed outlines of each seminar, or for more information, call Pencom at 1-800-247-8514

These are the most powerful and effective seminars in the industry. Ideal for meetings, trade shows, or any speaking/learning environment. Over 250,000 trained since 1987!

For:
- Owners
- Servers
- Trainers
- Managers
- Kitchen staff

Of:
- Restaurants
- Fast Food Operations
- Full Service Operations
- Institution Foodservice
- Hotels

Service That Sells! ... the Seminar

Based on the bestselling book
50 Guaranteed Ways to Improve Service, Increase Sales and Reduce Turnover in your Restaurant
Learn:
- How to increase your guest checks *$1 per person!*
- 63 ways to sell more appetizers, desserts and beverages
- 10 ways to increase business without advertising
- 12 ways to improve service
- How to energize your service and sales daily in less than three minutes
- 5 ways to improve training
- How to train host staff to sell
- How to remember guests names
- Why customers quit ... plus much more!

Award Winner 1991, 1992, 1993

Playing Games at Work
Creative incentives and contests to improve performance and profitability
Learn:

- 7 steps of designing effective incentives and sales contests for any department
- The difference between motivating tipped and non-tipped employees
- 27 effective ideas for waitstaff, kitchen and manager contests
- How to budget incentive programs ... plus much more!

Marketing From the Inside Out
Don't "Manage" your restaurant or bar ... Market it!
Learn:

- How to reduce your advertising budget 80% and double your customer traffic
- How to teach your entire staff to market your restaurant to their family, friends and classmates
- 29 ways to increase customer traffic without advertising
- How to "work a room" ... plus much more!

Energizing Your Management Skills

61 Ways to Improve Profit, Performance and Productivity

Learn:

- 14 ways to control costs and reduce waste
- 4 exercises that will improve teamwork instantly
- How to motivate the "burned out" employee or manager
- 21 ways to find, hire and retain quality employees
- The 10 steps of effective pre-shift team meetings
- How to motivate teen workers
- 12 Reasons your customers quit
- How to reduce labor, food costs ... plus much more!

Evolving With Your Customers

"You either change with the times or the times change you."

Learn:

- How the aging Baby Boomers will affect your business in the next 20 years
- 6 ways to differentiate your marketing to your three generations of customers
- How to adapt your menu to changing life-styles in the 90's and beyond
- The 17 "hot" food and beverage trends by the year 2000
- How to make your advertising appeal to your customers life-styles ... plus much more!

Award Winner 1992

Call 1-800-247-8514

Training video tapes ▪ ▪ ▪ ▪ ▪ ▪

Learn why successful companies like Marriott, Host International, Applebee's, Red Lobster, Chi-Chi's, Chili's and over 10,000 others worldwide use our videos to train their staff in the art of service excellence and suggestive selling.

Service That Sells! The Video

For your managers, waitstaff, bartenders greeters and busers. Putting it all together ... managing our cycle of service. A complete training program for the entire staff to maximize customer satisfaction and increase sales.

Learn:
- 10 ways to increase your guest checks $1 per person
- The 4 steps of service excellence
- 12 ways to identify your key customer contact points
- How to improve teamwork between servers and the kitchen
- Dozens of new ways to build performance, profits and productivity

Includes:
- 30 minute professional quality VHS video with Dolby™ sound
- Instructor Guide

50 Ways to Manage Service That Sells!

For managers, owners, operators, trainers and crew leaders. If you've ever caught Jim Sullivan's live seminars, you know why they are standing room only! Now bring Jim to your restaurant to train your staff any time with this new video. Over two hours of training!

Learn:
- How to increase your guest checks $1 per person
- 6 ways host staff can increase sales of appetizers and desserts
- The secret of the "Garbage Burger"
- 14 ways to reduce waste and control costs
- How to transform order-takers into salespeople
- 5 ways to eliminate Teflon Training (training that won't stick)
- 4 steps that will double your sales
- How to learn and remember guests' names
- 3 ways to deliver effective pre-shift team meetings. Includes Instructor Guide, plus much more!

CheckBUSTERS: The Art of Smart Selling!

For your managers, waitstaff, bartenders, greeters and busers. Here it is! Brand new for 1994! What if you train your servers to sell and they leave? What if you don't ... and they stay?! You asked for it — a sales training video for servers, bartenders and host staff that's realistic, relevant and gets results, instead of merely "covering content" — so you got it: *CheckBUSTERS: The Art of Smart Selling!*

Here's what you'll learn (and learn how to teach):
- How to transform order-takers into salespeople
- 3 steps that will immediately raise guest checks without raising prices
- How host staff can sell 20 bowls of soup each shift
- How to double appetizer and dessert sales
- How to raise guest checks as much as $1 per person
- How to learn and use your guests' names
- 4 steps of service excellence that customers demand
- How a $1 lotto ticket can increase gross sales $50,000 this year in your restaurant

- The secret of mastering menu ingredients and descriptions
- How to run effective pre-shift team meetings
- How much money you lose daily by *not* investing in CheckBUSTERS! Includes 1 comprehensive Instructor Guide plus Pencom's exclusive money back guarantee!

How to Sell More Beer

This innovative and entertaining 25-minute (approx.) video will show your waiters, waitresses and bartenders how to sell more draft and bottled beer, how to trade up regular beer to super-premium brands, how to up-sell draft beers to pitchers, how to pair up appetizers with beer and how to sell more non-alcohol brew. This video and instructor guide will transform your order-takers into a brew crew.

How to Sell More Appetizers

What's the first and best way to increase check averages? Sell your customers appetizers, soup or salads. This fun and informative video and instructor guide will show hostesses, servers and bartenders over 30 effective ways to increase your appetizer sales over 45% this year.

How to Sell More Wine

Available in April 1994

This fun and fast-paced video and instructor guide will show your servers, bartenders, managers and host staff how to double your wine and champagne sales by the glass and bottle.

Trainee Workbooks

Interactive workbooks, designed specifically for your servers, cover the major points of the videos and include a quiz to help you evaluate your server's comprehension of the material. Reinforce your video training for as little as $1 per person.

Training audio tapes · · · · · · · ·

Increase your restaurant and bar sales while you drive to work! Learn and earn with Pencom's three popular audiotapes.

Service That Sells! Live (2 tape set)

The only place in America where you can get an audio recording of Jim Sullivan's award-winning Service That Sells! seminar. This program will teach your managers and servers:

- 5 ways to improve training
- 91 ways to sell more appetizers, desserts and beverages
- How to train host staff to sell
- 10 ways to increase business without advertising
- How to remember guests' names
- 12 ways to lower monthly costs
- How to increase your guest checks $1 per person
- How to measure service excellence
- How to energize your service and sales in less than 3 minutes a day ... plus much more!

Playing Games at Work

How to implement successful employee contests, incentives and rewards. Once your staff is trained to better serve and sell, you'll need some practical ideas for effective server contests, rewards and incentives. That's what Jim Sullivan explains from A to Z in this award-winning audio. (Approx. 75 minutes)

- 7 steps of effective employee incentives
- 11 things you need to know before hiring anyone
- 5 ways to test the effectiveness of server sales contests

- How to get someone else to pay for your employee contest prizes
- How a $40 radio can increase a server's gross sales $600 per month
- How to budget sales contests for guaranteed return
- 15 server contest ideas

Want a great way to reinforce your video training?

... Look no more! Well, actually, lookie here! Audio adaptations of the following video programs are available:

- *Service That Sells!*
- *CheckBUSTERS: The Art of Smart Selling!*
- *How to Sell More Beer*
- *How to Sell More Appetizers*
- *How to Sell More Wine*

The Books

Service That Sells! The Art of Profitable Hospitality

Improve your profits, performance and productivity! For owners, operators, managers, servers, bartenders, speakers, vendors and chefs. The fastest selling book in food service history!

Learn:

- 67 ways to raise guest checks $1 or more per person
- 101 ways to sell more appetizers, extras, wine and desserts
- 14 ways to reduce costs
- 31 ways to transform order-takers into salespeople
- 6 ways to motivate teen workers
- 12 ways to improve your neighborhood marketing
- 26 ways to improve your service
- And much more!

New edition revised, expanded and updated in 1994, 208 pages, illustrated, appendix

Say What?! The 305 best things ever said about service, sales & supervision

We've been collecting quotes from restaurateurs and management "gurus" nationwide, across the country for the last ten years and have just published the best of the collection. Actions may speak louder than words, but quotable quotes speak volumes for the speechless trainer of manager. Knowing the exact expression, insight or clever remark to use can really add some "punch" to training sessions, lesson plans or meetings with your staff. Perfect for managers, team meetings, training sessions, manuals and reports. Makes a great gift, too!

Work Smarter — Not Harder!
The Service That Sells! Workbook

Available in April 1994

This dynamic interactive workbook is designed exclusively for your waiters, waitresses and bartenders. They'll learn over 327 different ways to improve service, increase sales and reduce costs. Based on the principles detailed in our best selling book *Service That Sells!* the interactive *Work Smarter — Not Harder! Service That Sells! Waitstaff Workbook* is guaranteed to show servers how to raise their guest checks a minimum of 25¢ per person or your money back, guaranteed. This fun-filled, award-winning, interactive workbook will make your current training manual obsolete and transform your order-takers into salespeople.

The 52 Best Hospitality
Incentives, Contests & Rewards

Available in April 1994

Once you've trained your staff to improve service, raise sales and control costs, it's helpful to have a wide variety of effective incentive and contest ideas that managers can use to motivate their staff to improve performance. So, here it is. The 52 absolute best (and most effective) incentive, contest and reward ideas sent in from some of the 30,000 readers of *The Service That Sells! Newsletter*. Wouldn't it be great to have 50 or more sales, service, safety, sanitation and supervision contest and incentive ideas at your fingertips? Order now ... and you will!

Guarantee

100% Customer Satisfaction. Guaranteed.
You don't like it? You don't pay.

At Pencom, our goal is 100% customer satisfaction, period! If for any reason our products, services or people fail to meet your expectations, let us know immediately by calling toll free at 1-800-247-8514. We will promptly fix the problem and immediately refund your original purchase price. We like to hear the good stuff, too. Let us know when one of our staff gives you that little extra *"Service That Sells!"* Also, if you have a training idea you'd like to share call us anytime.

1-800-247-8514

Thank you for choosing Pencom as your training partner!

Three easy ways to order • • • • • • • • • • • • •

Please clip or photocopy and mail or fax to *Service That Sells!*, P.O.Box 1920, Denver CO 80201 or fax to 1-800-746-2211 For immediate service call us at 1-800-247-8514.

1. Ordered by

Print name	Title

Company name	

Address (Please no P.O.Boxes)	This address is: ❑ Home ❑ Business

City	State	Zip

Telephone # (Required to process order)	Fax #

2. Ship to *(if different)*

Print name	Title

Company name	

Address (Please no P.O.Boxes)	❑ Home ❑ Business

City	State	Zip

Telephone # (Required to process order)	Fax #

3. Method of Payment

❑ I've enclosed check # _____ Payable to Pencom, Inc.

❑ Please charge to the following credit card:

❑ Visa *(13 or 16 digits)*   ❑ Discover *(16 digits)*

❑ MasterCard *(16 digits)*   ❑ American Express *(15 digits)*

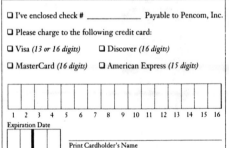

| 1 | 2 | 3 | 4 | 5 | 6 | 7 | 8 | 9 | 10 | 11 | 12 | 13 | 14 | 15 | 16 |

Expiration Date

Print Cardholder's Name

4. Order

Title	Quantity	Audio	Video	Unit Price	Total

5. Shipping and Handling

Continental U.S.

❑ **Standard Two-Day Delivery via Airborne Express**

All orders for in-stock items are shipped within 24 hours after we receive your order. Most orders will be delivered within 2 days of shipment. Add $4.95 for the first item and $1.75 for each additional item.

❑ **Guaranteed Next Business Day Delivery via Airborne Express**

Orders for in-stock items received by noon MST will be shipped that day and delivered the next day. Orders received after 12 noon will be shipped the next day and delivered within 24 hours of shipment. Add $9.95 for the first item and $1.75 for each additional item.

Call For Rates Outside the Continental U.S.

Merchandise total	
Shipping & handling *(see left)*	
Subtotal	
Colorado residents *(add 7.3% sales tax)*	
Grand total	